To Tamara

With Love

CODE OF THE THIRD
MILLENNIUM WARRIOR

Michael Corley

CODE OF THE THIRD MILLENNIUM WARRIOR

Tao of the Dragon Slayer

78 Lessons
To become a
Light Warrior

"The Light Warriors will be called upon in a time of Darkness and amnesia to step forward and represent what is best in humanity. The shadow, once exposed, will subside into the void from which it came. Here within lies the beginning of what has always been."

MICHAEL COLLEY

To order additional copies of this book, contact:
Xlibris Corporation
1-888-795-4274
www.Xlibris.com
Orders@Xlibris.com
22885

CONTENTS

Tao of the Dragon Slayer

**78 Lessons to
become a
Light Warrior**

Dedication and Prayer

I dedicate this work to my mother Rachel Colley.
Without her love none of this would have been possible.
She shared with me her creative spirit and from that,
I was forever changed.

Without mothers, our life givers, nothing would be possible.

A special thanks to the many souls that touched my life and
gave support to this manuscript.

Andrew Blagg
Shelly Giles
Traci Jordan
Alan Katz
Ean Kramer
Bryon Noel
Crystal Norigenna
Joe Perrone
Shimley Reynolds
Kathy West
Angie McClean
Cynthia Pararo
Dan Pittman

Dear Mother Teresa,

When you placed your hand to my head,
I gazed into your eyes and you touched my heart.
Thank you Mother Teresa for your blessing and your Light.
I will never forget the moment we met.

Michael

Thank you for a miraculous
example of compassion, sacrifice and love,
Mother Teresa (Agnes Bojaxhiu), you are
an inspiration to me and to us all.

On a September 5, Mother Teresa gracefully ascended
from an *Ambassador of Light* to a *Master of Light*.
This day will always be remembered in my heart as
"The day of the selfless act".

INTRODUCTION

In the time preceding this manuscript, I was a struggling artist living downtown in Atlanta, Georgia, less than a half a block from the eternal flame of Martin Luther King Jr. Strictly by happenstance, I encountered a wandering soul known only to me then as Dragon slayer. Largely humored and somewhat intrigued, I toyed with the relationship for some time. I soon realized that I had been chosen to understand and to illustrate the Dragon slayer's life and Warrior's Code. This Code, honored as Truth, was handed down by bloodline for thousands of years, awaiting the battle of the Third Millennium and the reawakening of the Light Warriors.

Draconis Interfectum was a Master of Light, which has no bloodline heir, therefore the knowledge was in danger of being forgotten. It was said; a new kind of warrior would emerge. This warrior would be empowered by light that shined from the heart. This light could extend from the chest as if it were a sword of Truth. This new kind of warrior is strong, without prejudice and would not be determined by race, creed, religion or gender. I was then led to understand that an Army of Light (sacred gathering of Light Warriors) would and must be united in order to combat the Ocean of Evil (shadow covering the planet). With all of my Americanisms, practicality and skepticism, I approached this idea with extreme caution. Having said all that, this is the **Code of the Third Millennium Warrior** & Tao of the Dragon Slayer. It is designed to empower and unite people with their warrior spirit. It is the awaiting truth that reminds us of a warrior's dignity that was once ours and can be reclaimed. If you listen carefully and hear a voice that states, "I want to help people, help the planet or just make a positive difference", then perhaps you too have heard the voice of the Light Warrior Spirit. These words have a gentle vibration of a master's voice. It is the master within your heart. This manuscript is designed to engage your real path and claim your real purpose. All this is possible if you want it. The challenge is yours to reawaken the sleeping lion and step forward into your power.

I consider it an honor to have been chosen to be a part of this undertaking. I only hope this adventure will empower your spirit as it did the warrior I came to recognize in myself.

Michael Colley

LIGHT

Light is clarity.

Clarity reveals Truth.

The Truth is what is real.

What is real?

"Love is real"

What is Love?

"God is Love"

God is Truth

God is Light

Through Love, Truth and Light,

we are all welcome

in the Kingdom of Clarity.

THE LIGHT WARRIOR PROPHECY

(A Battle of Light and Dark)

"The Lion will be called upon to awaken from its internal sleep, rise to face and meet the Dragons of Darkness on a battlefield. The battlefield is the soul and the field must be won for the lion to see its destiny. The lion's heart will evolve by the power of virtue and Light. The heart of the warrior will shape-shift and become a Warrior of the Heart. This will neutralize the Dragons and move beyond the internal battle to set an intention to balance the Darkness that has fallen upon the planet. The lion will gather other lions together as an army of Light Warriors to do battle with an Ocean of Evil. These lions, all equal and unified by a circle of Light will unite other circles until a great circle of Light covers the planet. The soul of the human body and the soul of the earth body will merge to become one and the same. The light will shine from the heart unto the great planetary shadow as if a great sword of truth emerged from the hearts of all Light Warriors. The Light Warriors will be called upon in a time of Darkness to step forward and represent what is best in humanity. The shadow once exposed will subside into the void from which it came. Here within lies the beginning of what has always been."

AUTHOR'S PROLOGUE

The Code of The Third Millennium Warrior is based on 78 lessons to becoming a Light Warrior. It was written with honesty, meditation, prayer, Akashic reading, Tarot interpretation, creative process, and more times than not, sitting for hours in a warm tub of water. The messages were clear and (I believe) to be from an angelic guidance that I call "A whisper in my ear." The Code of the Third Millennium Warrior is a way or path to a higher place. The focus of this manuscript is on our ancient gifts plucked from a memory recall and inspired by a constant guiding whisper. It speaks honestly and will repeatedly remind you that the warrior spirit is simply an applied effort within you. Whether you apply this God given spirit of effort to conquering by achieving or surrendering by letting go, the warrior spirit is yours to be accepted and developed. If you choose to take on this philosophy, know that you will embark on a sacred crusade. It will be a testament of honor and courage. It is not for those who must prove they are right but for those who choose they are Light. It is for those who find grace out of haste. This is a crusade to shift the mundane into fulfillment.

It was written as a tutorial and personal journal in the way that I received it. In its beginning, we must all take part in remembering we're walking a path of personal destiny. Destiny recall is necessary to seek out the reasons for one's true purpose. If you can find yourself, God will not be far. We are all holding space for our past, present and future selves. We are holding space for the planet. In this manuscript the student of the self steps out into becoming a teacher for others. We can be a beacon of light for others or accept and relive the mundane equations over and over again. Ultimately if we do not choose our higher path, we only return to the same mundane lessons. Life is a circle of Light, a circle of energy. If you do not finish what you started, you go round and round. The Code of the Third Millennium Warrior was recreated to aid our journey to Light.

Use it to become the Light Warrior you were meant to be, and then help unite us all in the power of your creation.

I was guided by visions and experiences to an understanding that Light Warriors were being chosen among us. These warriors were teachers of the new awakening and coming together in a sacred gathering or Army of Light. From this information the Light Warrior Circle was created to support the concept. The Light Warrior Circle is empowered to envelop the leaders of all love-based circles that have the clarity to see unity and the courage to set aside outdated differences. It was explained to me that the circles would merge themselves again and again until a great circle of light, filled with warriors of the heart, would cover the earth in a time of its greatest need. I was requested to document and convey this information in a manner that anyone who reads it would share the journey the way I did. I'm not asking you to trust my belief in these messages; all I ask is that you trust the honesty within yourself that the work triggers.

The journey begins with exploring the inner darkness and exposing the shadowy creatures that exist hidden from the Light. Hiding in the shadows is where your Dragons roam. The warrior spirit is a God-gift and ancient birthright to all human beings. It, like all God-gifts, must be claimed to be fully obtained. These warriors of Light will surface when darkness has caste a shadow upon the planet. The Light Warriors will step forward in the face of darkness and create Light with their hearts. They will represent what is pure in humanity. This was later confirmed for me in an ancient prophecy by the Maori tribe of New Zealand. In the Maori prophecy the mature Light Warriors will have the power to project twelve colors of light, each with a different application and known by the Maori as Rainbow Warriors or Light Warriors. There are similar prophecies told throughout North and South American tribes. I am not an expert in these prophecies. The information from this manuscript was documented long before I even heard of the tribal stories told of Warriors of Light coming in a time of human need.

I was completely unaware of these prophecies when this work began. I had completed the first draft of this manuscript, which I had been writing for well over a year. I had also already gathered nine Light Warriors together for an all night Light Warrior Circle held on the roof of a building in Atlanta, Ga. near the eternal flame of Martin Luther King Jr. I called this all night spiritual event the Gathering. Months later I was invited to a lecture being given by the late Maori Shaman Maki Ruka. It was then that he announced these prophecies to me for the first time. I stood up in a room filled with strangers in the middle of a lecture and asked him where this information came from. He told me that it was his tribe, the Maori's, and that he and his tribe had been waiting for 5000 years for the Light warriors to return. He then conveyed everything that I had already heard and written down from the whisper in my ear about a sacred gathering that would grow to 60,000 and beyond. This gathering would be the circle of Light Warriors. I conveyed on that day to this Shaman peace keeper of New Zealand in a room filled with strangers that I had been visited by this Light Warrior spirit and that I had been told to prepare the Gathering and do battle with an Ocean of Evil shown to me in a vision. In a room filled with onlookers I knew then that my destiny had unfolded. As strange as this sounds, you can't imagine how strange it was to speak it out loud. Maki Ruka and I later became friends and he was invited to witness an all night Light Warrior Circle gathering. The gathering is unencumbered by race, religion, creed, national origin or gender. All Warriors of Light sharing their paths and their gifts. Maki later told me he was old and tired of the journey and rested the responsibility of peace on me and others like me. He offered me many gifts from his travels and passed away shortly after. Since then the Light Warrior Circle continues to grow and through this manuscript will open new opportunities to find each other. Who they are and who they will be this time is anyone's guess. Possibly even within you exists the hidden memories necessary to unlock the power and the purpose to step forward as a humanitarian and continue on the path left by ascended masters. Perhaps you have the power, passion and purpose to finish what has to be done.

If so, may our hearts guide us to each other and gather as warriors with the respect of equals in a circle as it was foretold thousands of years ago.

Michael Colley

In reading this manuscript the question will be asked, "What is a Light Warrior and what is the Light Warrior Spirit?" The short answer is . . . if you have ever heard that little voice inside of you that says, "I want to help, I want to be a part of the solution, not the world's problem, if a voice inside of you is leading you to better yourself as a human being in a very small or large way, then perhaps you too are hearing the Light Warrior Spirit. Perhaps, you too are being called to serve as a humanitarian or a Light Warrior. This manuscript is dedicated to the spirit voice inside that wants to help us engage our real reason for being here.

"Truth is a great pool to swim the surface or dive the depths. Shallow may be the realization regarding one's self but deep is the reward of engaging the grandeur of one's true purpose."

LESSON ONE

The Time of the Remembering

This is the Code of the Third Millennium Warrior and a legacy for all things to come. Beyond this point there is strength with only the loss of your adolescence to contend. This may imply to a point of no return. Like the knowledge gained through pain, you cannot dismiss the power of its lesson. Once you remember your real self you are forever changed. All things are meant to be (which is not news), but is the opening dialogue that leads to the inevitable. As witnesses to the events at hand, this is your alarm, sounding in preparation for the message of fate. It is your fate that has brought you now to this rediscovered knowledge. Here in your hands is the truth of ancient secrets. This manuscript tells of a world born from memory of a time when men were kings and women possessed a richness that belonged to the magic of the True Earth. Men have always coveted this richness, but possession is a childish idea that should be remembered as a weakness. Strength lies in unity with a gentle balance between youth and wisdom, male and female. It was once thought to be lost; however, it has simply been waiting for its time again, "The time of the remembering". It is now here and at last the merging has begun. The gateways to unspoken images are at your fingertips. Masters long passed have waited for this gateway and are eager to complete their tasks. A teacher longs to teach, but only to willing students. These Masters of Light fight to find their vessels and return. Unlock your mind and dismiss the lessons of The Culture of the Forgotten Truth. **ENTER** into the newest age of yesterday, an era once forgotten but now again to be embraced. You have existed in the middle world between heaven and hell and between the lost and the again discovered. Many have simply forgotten their birthrights and others are waiting for someone to gift it to them; however, real knowledge is not learned, it is simply remembered. Come together now in the remembering of your destiny and the remembering of us all. Through your participation, know that you take part in the reunion of the whole. Depart from your childlike selfishness. Share in your responsibility and in your birthright. Journey beyond the surface of our shallow truth into the pool of deep truth. You will feel desires growing from the seeds of your earlier quest and remember the clarity that is necessary to balance conquering and surrendering. It is a true General and Peacemaker who can find victory between the two.

United by Light, we share our knowledge of all things. Together we have the conscious memory to complete a magnificent, collective puzzle, experience by experience. At present, this is an imagined idea. This thing termed imagination is the seed of a forgotten treasure. Imagination is what sets us apart from the creatures that roam in the dark and the driving force of the human experience. As the imagery grows clearer, more and more of your purpose will take hold. The Code of the Third Millennium Warrior is designed to engage that purpose, dissolve the mud from your uncertainty, and bring you closer to a strength and unity thought to be forgotten. You will explore the concept of Shape Shifting from what was to what should be. You will surrender a weaker self-concept to conquer a greater self-concept. You will un-block your light and expose your shadows. The result can be a balance of masculine and feminine within the self as well as the total union of all males and females, brother and brother, sister and sister, together and sharing their knowledge. Even the loneliest of souls has the ability to teach an experience, and a teacher has no distinction in social classes. All that is needed are the correct questions. The questions are as follows: are you ready to both teach and learn, without prejudice or prize? Are you ready to conquer the dark and surrender to the light? Are you ready to embark on a journey that will take you closer to your higher self? Are you ready to reawaken the sleeping lion? Are you ready to take responsibility for your true purpose and surrender blame? If you are ready to face the greatness of your greatest fear then it would appear, your time to fight has come.

LESSON TWO

Darkness

When our Light is blocked, a shadow projection is cast upon the surface of the soul. Blocked light casts a shadow on any or all dominions. The obstruction (Dragon) silhouettes the oblivion of amnesia. We forget our source clarity and our source creator due to this eclipse of Light. To recognize and remove the obstruction is the challenge of the Dragon Slayer. Challenging the realm of darkness is by far one of the most frightening of all the warrior's quests. Darkness is shielded by illusions that masquerade the very truth we require. To venture into the Darkness requires a distinct realization of the self; yet even self-clarity may not save you. Fear of the unknown is only the mystery of what lies ahead. It is here that life perpetuates its speed and moves us beyond linear time limitations. Here is where the Dragons await you. The lesson of your existence may lurk in the chambers down the hall; yet most people prefer to wait before moving forward. It is a common illusion to fear the unknown, as it is also common to fear your Greatness. Fear is fed to us during adolescence when we are too innocent and naive to combat its deception. We are plucked from the cradle and planted with seeds that linger in us until it's our time to fight. Fear is a Black Magic that keeps us all at bay never experiencing our potential. Without this illusion all men and women would achieve their highest goals and Darkness would lose its power in the Middle World. Understand this: for humanity, there is and has always been a battle of good and evil (The Game) in progression. To rise above this battle is your master key into ascension. For us who are having a human experience, we are merely members of a magnificent game of Chess in which we have the option of choosing the Light or choosing our Darkness. **Darkness is a**

consciousness void of Light designed to block potential. Our doomsday Armageddon reality is a part of that consciousness. A consciousness filled with Light and united to create an Army of Light will be necessary to neutralize the Armageddon prophecy. This power of free will, a glorious, God-given gift, is both lance and shield for a Light Warrior to wield. We all have a warrior spirit; unless you have forgotten you know how to fight. Because we possess the power to choose resistance deeply disturbs the very heart of all that is shadowy; however, even the Dark enjoys the challenge that this has brought to the Game. Darkness is as much a part of us as the Light, and is not all that difficult to evaluate. There is good and evil in every person. Study yourself and expose the obstruction that feeds your shadow within. Knowing your enemy is the mark of a seasoned and prepared warrior. To **"Know thy self"** is the clarity possessed by a **Defender of Light**. A Defender of Light dispels illusion. A **Dragon Slayer** faces fear doing battle with one's own Dark Dragons. Unfortunately, it is not nearly as simple as this sounds. Just as free will is a divine gift, this gift can be seduced away by what you welcome most. All God-given gifts can be corrupted because all divine gifts have a seductive shadow side. For example, love has its obsession, sensitivity has its vulnerability, self-confidence has its pridefullness, ambition has its greed, and the gift of making love has the darkness of betrayal looming over it. Be wary of psychics and seers without discipline because they too have been tempted by the shadow sides of their gift. This is the nature of the Game and the Game has its purpose. God is certainly above this battle of light and dark; however we having a human experience are not, yet. We must overcome our fears and obstructions to move forward and evolve. What is unfortunate for people is that **in the Dark, seduction is the weapon of choice**. Seduction is the core weakness inherited from the past to haunt human nature. Some will even welcome opportunities to face their self-destruction. Herein lies a testimony of human frailty, the very definition of weakness. Frailty, however, is not the mark of a warrior and is not the path that has led you to this manuscript. The Code of the Third Millennium Warrior will force you to take a stronger look at your attachment to seductions taught to you by the Culture of the Forgotten Truth. As a result, the pursuit of a deeper Truth along with the clarity to remain centered will remove the obstruction that your seductions would keep hidden in the dark. First we must agree, whether you fight to gain, fight to maintain or fight to let go, the ongoing lesson life continually teaches is, "We must Fight to Survive." This is a Warrior's Truth and Tao of the Dragon Slayer.

LESSON THREE

From Darkness to Light

Without Darkness we would not know Light. This reveals the cause and the effect, the Alpha and the Omega of our journey and mysteries. From Darkness to Light is the foundation for the seeker of Truth. It defines the journey and challenges to what lies ahead. It is said, "A journey of a thousand miles begins with a single step." Although this is true, a deeper truth is that even before the first step of a long journey there is "The correct question." For example: Who am I? Why am I here? Will I have the inner strength necessary to face and overcome what hides behind the darkest doors? Am I prepared to accept the Truth at the end of this journey? Do I have the balance and courage to move swiftly, without hesitation when battle challenges are necessary? Can I stay balanced and positive when all the negative forces of hell have ascended upon my path? It is the desire to answer the unknown that compels us to take that first step into new experiences. Who you were in the past, who you are right now and whom you are developing into, offer clues to the mysteries of a life purpose. An undivided past, present, and future is the story of self-realization. From beginning to now and beyond tells your personal story of moving from Light through Dark into Light. From creation to creation is the circle of Light. Knowing yourself helps secure divine purpose that produces the ability to reach higher levels towards the light of God. To know yourself as a creator brings access to higher rewards along the path to achieve higher self-awareness. This requires imagination combined with a strong sense of your personal right vs., wrong, and Light vs. Dark. To overcome the battle of Light and Dark (The Game) you must first learn the rules. A personal moral code must be achieved by clearly defining what you believe by the meaning of the word "WRONG." To define the meaning of "WRONG" is not that difficult, in fact, it is simple. "WRONG" is the opposite of what you believe to be "RIGHT." If you believe a person should be faithful to their mate, then your infidelity will lead you to inner conflict. If you believe that people shouldn't take what doesn't belong to them, and you are met with the temptation to steal, you must make the choice. Ask yourself, will I represent the right or will I represent the wrong of who I believe I am or should be. Without this understanding of our personal rights and wrongs, uncertainty occurs which leads to hesitation, which leads to seduction, which leads to denial, which leads to defeat. "Defeat" is a term given to those who have lost the gift of choice. There are some who believe that there is no such thing in spirituality as right and wrong. It is true that God is beyond the battle of Light and Dark, however, we are not. It is this battle or Game within ourselves that perpetuates the journey toward higher light and eventual ascension. **The line drawn by right and wrong establishes a core law (personal truth), which you identify as the "self".** Denial of your core self will only lead to internal imbalance. The distance we stray from our core laws can create two opposing armies in a self-conflict. Conflict of the self is far more dangerous than an adversarial face off. Any battle that takes place with a faceless enemy will manifest fear and become a total threat to peace. Any battle that takes place in a nonphysical realm, will undoubtedly transform your world from one dimension to another. Dimensional shifts are how the dragons of fear, seduction and addiction emerge to take physical shape. Inner conflict will deliver external problems to your front door. Disrespect or disregard of your core laws will bring the enemy closer. Allowing the enemy into the house is always a dangerous strategy that requires clear thinking and careful planning. Poor planning is the first indication of defeat. Disregarding clarity (Light) is the opening ceremonial magic of Dark manifestation. Some even welcome their self-destruction. This sabotages the path causing a deadlock. The game is Life and the journey to Light has not yet been completed. Until it is, we are both Light and Dark beings seeking balance. The direction of your journey is up to you. You will at times manipulate your darkness, justifying it for pleasure, fun or maybe just boredom. If your dark manipulations manifest into a life intention, the path of the Light Warrior becomes blocked. Darkness only has the power you give it. This is part of the free will gift and important playing rules in the Game. Be honored to have a role in the Game. Without you the great Mother of us all would have one less warrior, one less beacon of Light.

LESSON FOUR

The Child Within

Creation is the creative process. Creation begins for us with innocence. Our innocence has the tremendous power of freedom. Paradoxically freedom is also a primary motivation for warriors in battle. The lack of freedom and a thirst for knowledge takes us away from our childlike innocence. It stands to reason that being free and being childlike can bring us joy and allows us a greater understanding of our inner self. Being childlike can also offer us an appreciation of the greater powers that reside over us. What could be greater than to experience the childlike awe of a magnificent sunset, a beautiful waterfall or the brilliance of a well-orchestrated symphony? We are all children of sorts. We are children of God, children of the earth mother, and children of our own parents. Being childlike reminds us of our truth, our virtue and our time of pure innocence. Nurturing the child within for healing has merit; however, it must only be recognized as a temporary strategy in an ongoing mission. In time, all children grow. This is a natural law and thinking otherwise can lead to self-indulgence. Maturity speeds up development under nature's law, but this is up to you. You have more power than you know and a delay of responsibility will burden the world around you. Innocence is a wondrous gift, but in time we are all called upon to assume the responsibility of our parental-selves and claim our birthrights. In claiming our parental-selves we must ask the question, will I lead, will I follow or will I stand-alone? In choosing, purity will undoubtedly embody a source of strength and simplicity. A virtuous hero is an ancient ideal that still possesses charm. A virtuous warrior is the least conflicted and therefore has greater access to his or her powers. Innocence without maturity, however, requires patience, nurturing and guidance. If naive to the illusions of Darkness you will manifest a lesson for your maturity. Eventually children must learn to become parents and the parent must remember to be a child. Do not give up the play that is childlike in all of us; however, when its time for battle, put the children to bed. A warrior must recognize opportunities to improve survival. This may seem harsh, and yet, it is the essence of the Warrior's Truth. Life itself is the constant teacher of maturity. It is true that nurturing one's child self for healing has value, but only because it is understandable that freedom may be necessary in the process of healing. Healing is the child clinging to the mother nurturing us and connecting us to the spirit of the Earth Mother. Healing is time well spent. Taking time to heal is not a defeat. It is a sabbatical. A good General never leads an army of wounded and defeated men into battle. Understanding the value of rest and recovery may be a necessary strategy to attain the victory you desire. No warrior can maintain performance without appropriate recovery. However, too much sabbatical can lead to ruin. Healing is much like the pursuit of one's core self; you must remove layer by layer the burdens from your life until the truth is free. Thus, become the sculptor who chips away the stone to free the image beneath. Break free from the unnecessary burdens that bind you. If you are still in recovery, then try training for the glory of a greater day. As long as a plan of action prevails, there is hope. The three things to remember are: to choose life, choose strength, and choose not to live in fear. In short, a warrior must fight to live well. The result may amaze even you. The Culture of the Forgotten Truth has distorted your self-image. Your culture has taught you that it's acceptable to live in fear, stressed by a thing that only you can beat. No matter how hard your life is the lessons of your battles are here for you. Lessons are our parents. They are here to challenge and teach you. Stress is created by the positive and the negative in friction. Stress is your very own beautiful, bloodthirsty Dragon to slay. It denies freedom, frightens us and takes us out of balance. Stress declares war on peace. Your cultural protocol would have you accept it, or ignore it. Your culture has shown you what to believe and how to coexist with the Dragon. In retrospect, if you believe you should live in fear, you will. If you believe you are a child you will be a child. If you believe you are a victim, you are. If you believe your life is not of any fault of yours, then you have denied your maturity. If being a child makes sense then you will need to play out this idea. Unfortunately the child in you believes that your Darkness manipulates you, but it does not. The Master within you understands that we manipulate our Darkness. We choose our seductions and sometimes become lost in the experience. The child within plays mischievous games and then blames others for mistakes and misfortune. The warrior within accepts the responsibilities of playing too close to the edge of dangerously Dark realms. The Truth is that being a child is an important part of the journey. It is the beginning potential of the greatest life story ever told. The deep truth is being childlike means little in the heat of battle. Notice both statements are truths that seem to almost contradict each other. Only together do they make the most sense. Being a child is an important part of the journey but sometimes we must set aside the child and fight. The child and the warrior have their purpose. We must all seek the deepest truth possible because attach one truth to a lie and people will follow their seductions into hell and to the slaughter. Innocence is only the first part of the journey and as children we have the ability to dismiss our worries to the point of delaying or even denying our destiny. Children can dismiss but warriors overcome. The warrior spirit is a birthright, but it can be seduced away with words. Your experience, no matter how horrid, has value. It's up to you to find value, understand it, shape it, use it and grow beyond the victim. Healing offers us the gift of veteran experience. Healing yourself will recall your original quest to overcome your fears. You will recall your higher purpose, and your unclaimed inheritance. If the strategy of surrender is more beneficial to win the battle with Darkness, then remember to call upon acceptance. Choosing surrender and being defeated are as different as having the choice to accept (surrender) or having a choice taken away from you (defeat). You may find that the child within you may not have the maturity to let go. You may find it is the mature warrior within you that has the strength to surrender and move on. **It is the fire from a candle that produces the light.** In God's Light balancing youth and wisdom, we shine. This is your birthright and a rite of passage into maturity. The warrior spirit is ancient. You are a child of God and are entitled to this gift. With it you can overcome impossibility, change reality, and forge a path that will take you as far as you have the courage to explore. Embrace your warrior-self as you would embrace your child-self. They are both a part of our journey. They are both necessary in the evolution of the human experience, and after all, they are both within you.

LESSON FIVE

Win or Lose

A gambler's code dictates that for every winner there is a loser and for every loss something can be won. The core nature of the human spirit strives to be a winner. This is perpetuated from birth to death with little alteration of the theme. With winning comes victory along with responsibility that requires discipline. With every loss, illusion is set aside to relinquish false images of possession. Winning and losing together are designed to offer what you need, but not always what you want. The Culture of the Forgotten Truth would have you believe that winning is the only course of action. Acquiring and acquiring until there is nothing left to own. This idea can create the imbalance of victory that exists within a shallow truth. Shallow truth occurs when a lie is attached to a Truth. This leads millions of partially informed individuals to believe that if A and B are true, then C must also be true, when in fact, C could be evil itself. This is the deception of propaganda, used for thousands of years to misdirect and enslave the human spirit. Massive belief structures are founded on this sort of deceptive manipulation. Is prosperity "how much you can make" or "how well you can live"? Loss can serve us positively; however, the negative blocks most people's vision. Within the negative we can find positives as well as within the positive we can find the negatives. Unchecked negativity can manifest blame, which is a virus that easily attaches itself to loss. Blame is the primary affliction of the victim. Blame has weakened humanity since the beginning of our existence. Blame is the manifestation of "Original Sin." Men and women, brothers and sisters must recognize that we are divided by a cultural protocol that lies by casting blame to what is lost. Our most ancient teachings, such as the parable of Adam and Eve, would lead followers to believe that the woman's role was to mislead man's spiritual endeavor. Man's misinterpretation of this story has only misled us from the Truth. With a deeper perspective, the story tells that Adam was incomplete without Eve, indicating they were both created by God to help each other. Masculine and feminine balance is a holy and sacred union through most western and eastern philosophies. In the Old and New testaments, the Garden of Eden was a complete paradise during the union of Adam and Eve. Only later paradise is seduced away by one dark choice and then another. People are quick to believe God was an unforgiving God rather than to accept that men and women blaming each other for their weak behavior could cause the end of a harmonious situation. From this story blame perpetuated itself and created mass social dogma that supported religions based upon man above woman or woman against man. This grew into religions blaming other religions, people against each other until differences create war. Clearly we can read that paradise occurs when a man or a woman feels complete. Was disobeying God's word unforgivable or was blaming each other truly the original sin that cast men and women into millennia of separation? From religion, to politics, to courtrooms, to backyard outings you have accepted lies attached to the belly of a Truth, much like a hiding shadow attaching itself to your body or a dark remora scavenger under the belly of a shark. Blame declares that it is not our fault and that we have no control, no responsibility and no power. "We were powerless." This idea has weakened us all. However, a warrior maintains control by taking responsibility for losses. A Defender of Light dispels illusion and brings greater depth to a shallow truth. The Culture of the Forgotten Truth would have you exist in shallow Truth and blame, never leading you to the pool of deep Truth. The deep Truth is that to completely gain you must acquire without attachment. Absolute possession is a childish idea that breeds greed, envy, jealousy and a number of other Dark Dragons. You must learn to receive with no need to give and give with no need to receive. A gift is to be given and then **forever let go**. If anything is expected from a gift, then the gift-giver is manipulating a hidden barter and not giving at all. If the gift is love, be aware that it can be tainted by shadowy expectations for manipulated returns. Again, you must give the gift (love) and then let it go. To give with the expectation that your needs will be served is not giving at all. If you are offering your love and fear losing what you have offered, this too is defeating your purpose. To fear losing what you've gained invites oppression. **Freedom is always the primary goal,** i.e. freedom to mate, freedom to live, freedom to remember what is real, and of course the freedom to love who you really are. Unfortunately, freedom cannot be completely attained if you allow the fear of loss to exist. The fear of loss is an insecurity and weakness. A warrior would not choose a strategy that breeds weakness. **This is not to say that one should not fight for what he or she has.** On the contrary, but if what you've attained imprisons you, you are not free and may be fighting for the wrong thing. A Defender of Light fights from a pure heart with serious intentions. Great wealth tempts us all. Wealth can bring us freedom, but obsession on wealth will manifest greed. Greed is a bloodthirsty Dragon of Darkness. He sits lurking over the very seduction that you would more than welcome through your door. Take note, if you welcome the Dragon into your house then you must accept the consequence of your actions. Our seductions are never far away. Your choices may unwittingly bring you head on with the great corrupter of souls. **FEAR, SEDUCTION and ADDICTION are the Dragons.** These three are the unholy trinity. They are you and your poorest desires, but if you have Virtue over the Dragon there is hope. The battle of Light and Dark (The Game) is ongoing. In the Game, balance is the prize that will take you to the next level. As long as there are lessons and students, the game of life continues. You may believe you deserve your seductions, but not if the Dragon has control. The power you use to win is important. Do you win well or do you invite seduction? Have you formed an alliance with the Dragon? Does the face of your greed, envy, selfishness or stress help you succeed? If so, this is a dangerous strategy. Ask yourself if your life has balance: Can you give and receive, teach and learn, win and lose well? Can you be attached and also detached? If you care only about winning, then prepare for what is coming and for what has to be done. The Dragon is alive and your strategy affords you a grand fight with a great adversary. The battle for your soul plays a huge role in sustaining your free-will destiny. The lion (warrior) and the dragon will meet on the battlefield. This is a challenge that even the ancient Masters find worthy and rewarding. So take a determined stance. Grip your sword because it can save you. Take a deep breath and remember that to move freely, you must relax the very thing you are holding onto so tightly. This is the balance of possession.

LESSON SIX

The Word

"In the beginning there was the Word." The power of the word is so immense that it can unlock the deepest secrets of your life. In this manuscript of rediscovered words, The Code of the Third Millennium Warrior has diagrammed the truth in words to help you merge the warrior spirit with Light. To engage this concept we must understand and trust the language necessary to proceed. This merger of one's warrior spirit and spirituality is a quest for Truth. Because it is a common belief that we get what we give, the seeker of Truth must accept that the discipline of honesty leads to a fortune in Truth. So many people mislead themselves by believing that one can seek the Truth without having to be completely honest. This is why so few find fulfillment. For that reason let's begin with defining what is in a word.

There is a growing belief that spirituality will overthrow religion. This is a battle of words. "Spirituality is the experience of God, and religion is the word of God." Why is a battle of words so necessary? Unfortunately in a time of empowered Darkness, we have become jaded, believing words can lie or be simply misinterpreted. If religion is the word and words can lie, where will you place your faith? This is a question for many seekers. A lack of faith in words causes confusion. Confusion leads to seduction, which can detour your path. How do you find love if the words make you angry? Language is tricky. Many people manipulate it. It is sometimes difficult deciding the best choice for this reason. Sometimes we only trust what is more fashionable at the moment. Clarity of self is essential to empower your choices. Understandably, life is a trial and error process that will yield to study. Choosing to analyze is a strategy. No one prefers to be indecisive. **It's** important not to wander aimlessly in your pursuit of spirituality, especially when religion can help you find it. This entire dialogue is to illustrate a slippery thing known as the "Word." The power and influence of words are enormous. The "Word" has been prostituted to the highest degree, yet retains its unique ability to deliver the most touching and profound Truth. Such flexibility is miraculous because it proves time and again, it is willing to caravan to both heaven and hell. Language is a remarkable tool to utilize, especially considering with extreme circumstances it is capable of saving life or evoking death. It can carry the gift of spoken love or the evils of Dark betrayal. It can open the gates of hell, and it can welcome you into the kingdom of heaven. When spoken in love the power and virtue of Light shines. Each time words are spoken for evil, hate, or betrayal, they champion the darkest cause. The Ocean of Evil grows more powerful, possibly, with some unconscious aid from your voice. This lesson is not to judge, but to make known the power of our language.

Here is the first challenge and your chance to make a spiritual stand as a Defender of Light: **You must become as true as your word.** To support deception with your words contradicts your quest for Truth. You must stand for Truth and defend the Truth, which all begins by **telling the Truth.** If your words are not honest you have deceived only yourself. **Liars create an imaginary world in which they believe that the people they lied to believe those lies.** Most people do not believe a lie at the moment it's told, but without evidence to the contrary, avoid conflict and play along. Lying only reduces your self-image and limits your potential for Truth. "In the end all Truths will be realized," and all deceptions require a price. From this day forward, if you wish to become honored, you are called upon to live by your word. **Without honesty there is no honor in your words.** This is not easy and does not mean you must be brutal. It may mean putting forth an effort to find a kinder way to deliver your honesty. When you are known for the integrity of your word, people describe you with other words such as ethical, honorable or reliable. Your opinion becomes prized and respected. You will walk head high amongst respected people, knowing clearly that you belong with noble company. In time, your word will carry weight, and have influence and power. A Defender of Light dispels lies because your word is a Sword of Truth that cuts through delusion. Your words can expose Darkness to Light. A shift will occur as false images fade. If you live and speak honestly you will represent the voice of Truth. **To Speak the Truth is the first of nine challenges for the Light Warrior.**

LESSON SEVEN

Masters of Light

A Master of Light is an ascended being. There is no such thing in the physical world as a true spiritual master. Spirit and body are two different worlds in a symbiotic relationship. **A spiritual master exists beyond the physical body.** However, the gateways are now open, messages are being transmitted and you have an inherited recall to listen. A voice can be heard when all is still. It is a voice of your guiding light. Masters of Light are open channels to apprenticeships. Masters of Light choose people as vessels and unlock their minds. To be guided along the Master's Path is a great honor. Masters of Darkness will also engage you along the way. It is you who will determine the direction of your fate. Some reach the journey's completion in this life cycle. Others will choose a slower resolve. When finished we will go with God. There are many levels to attain spiritual mastery and ascension. The Code of the Third Millennium Warrior will guide you through the primary seven.

The Master's Path

7th Mastery:	*The Master of Light (ascension)*
6th Peacemaker:	*The Ambassador of Light*
5th Messenger:	*Tao of the Warrior Priest / Priestess*
4th Healer:	*Tao of the Light Warrior*
3rd Warrior:	*Tao of the Dragon Slayer*
2nd Self:	*My way, "I am . . ."*
1st Creation:	*The Creative process*

The Master's Path is a quest for Truth and therefore must begin with honesty. The words you choose will have power. Many people will claim mastery in your lifetime and there will be many false prophets. To claim mastery of a subject implies the completion of learning, which implies that teaching is the only course of action. However, the game is life and the journey has not yet been completed. If a teacher passes on knowledge to a student, this is the natural law of progression. A teacher should not claim mastery of one discipline and simply disregard all the others. The very thought conjures the imagery of imbalance, and imbalance contradicts the image of a master. However, a master's status can be given in ceremony as a gift, as an acknowledgment of achievement or simply as praise and compliment. This should be claimed only as a material trophy and never as a sincere testament of self. Claimed in arrogance, the ego is deluded and further representation of balance becomes false. Teaching and learning together create the forum in which Truth is remembered and this is the fabric of all relationships. With every new encounter of souls, a question should be asked, "Am I the teacher or am I the student?" In time this will become natural. Honesty and sensitivity are required for the answer to present itself. If uncertain, do not become discouraged because the technique will grow stronger in time. The teachers that taught you accepted that to teach is an honor and a responsibility, and so should you. Have faith that the master within will guide you. Upon reflection, if you are the teacher for another human being, know your obligations and represent yourself sincerely. After all, it may be that your honesty is the lesson. Honesty is wholly important. A false representation of yourself will dim the light of virtue that being a teacher brings. Do not worry over trivial details. A higher force has created this relationship. Trust in your inner guiding voice and have faith in the exchange of Light. If, on the other hand, you are the student in this encounter, take a deep breath and absorb your lesson. This is inherently more difficult because the strategy of surrender is necessary. You have not been taught the value of surrender because you have been distorted by The Culture of the Forgotten Truth. However, the power to let go is strength, not weakness. The "strategy to surrender" is every bit as powerful as the "strategy to conquer." Letting go demonstrates the flexibility of a mature warrior. To let go of your arrogance and pride will allow you to move easier throughout the learning process. **We are all students at times.** The only dismissal of your responsibility to learn is the death of your physical body. If your teacher is strong in one science but weak in another, then learn only what is required. Do not dismiss all of his or her information because you have passed judgment on a weakness. There is a joy in knowing that a student possesses the ability to grow beyond a teacher's weakness. Do not block your own learning process. Even the healthiest soul can learn from an unhealthy soul. Defying this belief or claiming the false title of "Master" may cause you to pass by an opportunity to learn the very thing you need. Those who claim to need nothing have disregarded their responsibility to accept and learn. If "knowledge is power" then choosing ignorance is weak. Choosing to be weak is not the mark of a warrior. When a weakness manifests it is of the utmost importance to a warrior not to ignore it. Darkness is the champion for weakness. Expose the weakness through the clarity that Light provides. In the Light, **define the Dragon as a fear, seduction or addiction**. Determine clearly your fear because fear is the body of the Dragon. Choose your ground and your weapons wisely because from this point on you must understand who you are and who you choose to be. Call in all the protectors in your lineage and spirit world. The Masters of Light have many names such as Abraham, Christ, Mohammed, Buddha and Mother Earth Spirit, etc. Listen to your guiding voice. A Defender of Light seeks Light out of Darkness. A Defender of Light accepts there are no mistakes, only lessons to learn and tests for those lessons learned. A Defender of Light cannot be defeated. Defeat only casts a shadowed illusion for those who choose to look back rather than facing forward into Light. Look ahead gracefully. The breath will help you find acceptance. Breathing gives us life and generates a more graceful clarity. The breath is essential to communicate with heaven and earth. The game is life and breathing manifests a peaceful life through natural magic. Trust your instincts and move in the direction that feels correct. If you choose to be a Slayer of Dragons, face your fear and fight with courage. This is the way it has always been and is today according to the ancient Masters of Light.

LESSON EIGHT

The Seductress

The game of life is a drama riddled by our dilemmas between seduction or virtue. In every moment there lives a choice. In every choice there is both Light and Dark; these are the healthy or unhealthy consequences to our decisions. Most choices are simple and mundane, but never underestimate the value of a choice. Thousands upon thousands of choices, from the basic to the extreme, may culminate in nothing more than a decision to go to bed. Hopefully, the healthier choices will balance out the unhealthy ones. Also we can't discount our choice to make no choice at all. Our healthy directions are determined by the distance it transports us into clarity. Our unhealthy choices are determined by the opposite of our highest Light. The unhealthy direction, conversely, will lure you with seduction and offer you a guide to darker realms. It can offer you sensations and temptations as if it were some mystical Seductress. It is seductive magic that leads us into mechanical behavior. **Unconscious mechanical behavior** is what keeps our Dragons hidden in the dark. Expose the behavior, expose the Dragon and you can confront, release or starve the life force of the Seductress. Attack the pattern and therefore "Attack the plan" of seduction or addiction.

We all possess a Seductress. The Seductress is the shadow side of desire. It lures us under the pretense of healing, but with the intention to enslave. In our youth temptation is unbridled by a lack of life experience and carves a path deep inside our behavior. These seductive desires create poor patterns or nonproductive habits. These habits become the burden of our later maturity as our wisdom forces us to deal with the inevitable consequences of our seductions. Whether through lust, fear, rage, greed, envy, pride, laziness, deceit or gluttony you will always have the Seductress to distract you. The key is to empower your Light by choosing virtue. Light exposes what you need and the Light is infinite. You have barely tasted your true potential. Take from the Light all you feel you deserve and then take ten thousand times more. You cannot exhaust its supply. Fear will block your memory but you cannot deny your evolution forever. Eventually, the universe will force you to take action because action is the natural state of the universe. Nothing except change remains constant and keeping things as they are is a futile task. You have been given free-will gifts along with a warrior spirit, merge the two and you can change to your liking. Out of the thousand choices in a day it only takes one to overcome your seductions and emerge changed for the better. The opposite choice is a darker path where self-destruction or destiny damage may await you.

Once there was a good man who had all the potential of love and kindness. He saw in his mind the ideal man, and he worked diligently to become that man. He loved his mate and tried to do what was expected of him. Unfortunately, he was seduced in his youth by his temptations and misguided social protocol. His cultural misdirection whispered masculine ideology and his temptations supported it. A pattern formed and, at the expense of his soul's journey, he became too weak to fight it. Though he loved his mate he could not remain faithful, and his Seductress led him down a dark path where his greatest Dragon awaited. Unarmed, without Light or warrior spirit, the Dragon devoured him and he lost everything. He lost his love, his Light, and his soul to a thing that he embraced rather than fought. Unfortunately, sometimes **"The Dragon will have its day."** Do not mistake sex for sexual healing. Sexual healing is sacred. It requires discipline and clarity to shift the seductress into Light. Be wary of what is too good to be true. Temptation is the doorway to seduction and is a great adversary. The man spoken of deluded himself into believing that he could create Love on one side of town while simultaneously creating betrayal elsewhere. Love is Light, Betrayal is Dark, and the two are extremely opposite. To play both realms of Light and Dark is a fool's strategy. Too many fallen warriors have tried to play this foolish game, only to be devoured. Take a single moment and make a healthy choice. A healthy choice is the beginning to exercising responsibility. The discipline of the warrior spirit will emerge. If you mirror your life's intention by your seductions then you have even betrayed yourself. If, however, you are strong and embrace the Defender Of Light status, infinite victory and union await your arrival.

LESSON NINE

Dragon Slaying

Fear is the body that breeds the Dragon. They feed with negative energy devouring your positive intent. Dragons run blockades between your vision and your memory. After blocking Light a shadow causing amnesia occurs. The Dragon seduces us into the shadow where we can completely lose sight of our Light. Sometimes we become lost in the shadow and forget our way back. This is the cloaking system of shadow designed to manifest amnesia. When we forget what we are we become easy targets for seduction or addiction. Dragons may have different faces, but the energy is negativity such as hatred, rage, or fearful stagnations. Our free flowing Love, Light, and Truth, are a constant except when they seem to be forgotten. If you can accept that fear is at the core of evil and that God is Love, then you have exposed the two great adversaries of Light and Dark. God is above the battle of Light and Dark, but Evil is not. The decision to choose virtue defines **Dragon Slaying**. It is replacing what is negative with what is positive to create a balance. Since the beginnings of time these two antagonists (seduction and virtue) have waged a war for our choices, playing out their battle within the hearts of every person. Darkness continues to seek victory by blocking Light; however, **Light needs only to be embraced. Virtue then moves us to the next level where balance occurs to create peace.** Our soul is striving to reach God as our higher self. With each life choice made with loving intention, the **power** of virtue comes to our aid. Our virtue moves us to the next level where we have the power over our seductions from the past level. Once stabilized in the new level of awareness, we come to find we can balance our virtues and our seductive desires of the past. Balance is the prize and the essence of Tao. **Tao of the Dragon Slayer** is the third and a very powerful level to spiritual mastery. At the third level the warrior gift is claimed and with it, fear can be overcome. Fear is an imagined judgment, not born of creation that blocks our path. God did not create fear. Fear is a manifestation of the darkest part of Mankind's imagination. It is a fantasy designed to entrap us, as are all the nine seductions. Fear comes from a deep and dark place. Most people will not even allow themselves a chance to deal with it directly, so we reshape it negatively into anger, prejudice or insecurity. Fear is negative essence. The greater the essence a Dragon can establish, the more magnitude its damage has in the middle world. Fear is your imagination's shadow manifested to bring negative drama to you and your world. Fear causes weakness by denying or forgetting your source Light. Human beings have a self-destruct mechanism called sabotage. We draw upon sabotage when we devote ourselves to weakness. Sabotage is unnatural and the opposite of nature's laws for survival. Self-destruct mechanisms are programmed behaviors. Your birthright to fight gives you power for survival during weak experiences. When we lose this power we feel lost, yet we often freely give it away. Why? The Culture of the Forgotten Truth teaches a philosophy of self-victimization. **Victimization is a virus.** A virus is a species that will kill its host. This dark virus will feed on you and devour your power. Open your eyes and heart because you have been altered by a cultural protocol to blame. Blaming has weakened you. When blaming, you are announcing that you had no choice, no responsibility and no power. Why would anyone give away power so easily? The Code of the Third Millennium Warrior is designed to aid you in seeing through illusion so you can maintain your power and then "Follow your heart." If fear is not created by light, is it real? When is a masquerade ever real? When blinded by victimization you can twist reality to see what your seductions want you to see. The Dragon Slayer must look beyond fear to face and overcome the Nine Spiritual Dragons of Seduction. This means taking on a conscious battle to achieve balance with:

The Nine Spiritual Dragons of Seduction

1. **Anger**—Rage based on ill will with blind concern for a compassionate solution
2. **Pride**—Pride-ful resentment based on the belief that "I" am better than another
3. **Deceit**—Addiction to misconduct or masquerade, false representation, dishonest
4. **Envy**—Desire for what is unattainable, jealous wanting of what others have, ungrateful
5. **Greed**—Desire for more than is needed, selfishness
6. **Fear**—Imagination turned against oneself, distorted projection of what is real
7. **Gluttony**—Desire to overindulge pleasure or pain, addictive nature
8. **Lust**—Obsession, extreme careless wanting, the essence of seduction and desire,
9. **Sloth**—Denial of spirit, loss of will and intention, depression, lazy, action problem

One by one you must claim your virtue by slaying these nine dragons. It takes clarity, courage and compassion to face your shadow.

A Dragon Slayer has three basic choices when facing an overwhelming foe:

First, *he or she can choose to face and fight through the challenge, thus using the **conquering** strategies.*

Second, *he or she can choose to face the challenge by letting it go, walk away, stop caring, releasing the dragon and* *forever the burden from their world, thus using the* **surrendering** *strategies.*

Third, *is for the most difficult addictions. The third strategy is for the monsters. The one you cannot best from your present vantage point. This strategy is used when you cannot conquer it or let go of it; therefore you must starve the dragon until it weakens. To beat it you must cut off its dominance, thus deny its negative power source and its ability to wreak the havoc of impending devastation. It is a choice to accept that your adversary is greater than you for now, but through dedication and patience one can break all addictions and* **neutralize** *even a monstrous dragon. In time, a weakened dragon faced with the evolved warrior's determination can offer another day to conquer or surrender it away. Faith is the* **weapon of neutralization.**

To be a Dragon Slayer is a noble and honorable profession. Those who wish to be greater choose it. Consider who you are now and who you would be if you overcame all your fears and addictions? Your ancestors await your response. Take this moment of Truth to answer them honestly. The Light Warrior conviction is to overcome Darkness and teach others to do the same. You, as a warrior for Light, have an obligation to slay your own personal Dragons and resume your destiny. Memory within your imagination blocked by darkness holds the key to your true destiny. Your memories will flow like water when you remove the blocks keeping you forgetful. Ask yourself if you can materialize honor and bravery? Virtues are developed through alchemy. Are you secure enough to choose humility over pride, compassion over judgment, honesty over a false image that would make people admire you? Could you fight without anger, without malice, and without fear but instead with pure intention? To face a Dragon with fear or anger will only feed it. You must surrender your negative seduction and become more positive. Dragon Slaying is a paradox. It is a Chinese finger puzzle. The Dragon Slayer understands you must surrender to conquer and conquer to surrender. This is your invitation to take arms against the shadowy illusive monsters of your personal crusade. Break free to be free.

LESSON TEN

The Correct Question

Who is the Dragon Slayer? There has always been a warrior class in every major civilization since the beginning of time. Action applied towards victory is a mandatory element of human evolution. We must acknowledge and accept that human beings were bred with the instinct to fight. The warrior instinct reminds us of who we really are; this is apparent most during disaster. **The warrior spirit is the essence of will power and purpose.** This essence has had many names and has taken many shapes. It is with us and within us. If seduced by our shadow we will use our warrior spirit for destruction. If used correctly we will fight for Light as well as self-preservation. When necessary, the human race has proven time and again, we can and will make a stand. It is our nature and our birthright to survive. The Dragon Slayer is in the wolf, the lion and the bear. It is in our champions, our sports heroes, and in the common people who rise up against the odds to come to our rescue. Even our concepts of divine spirits, such as Archangel Michael, are revered as a warrior class in heaven that allows us to understand that indeed angels are Defenders of Light. Michael represents a warrior spirit combined with the Light of God. It is with his guidance, inspiration and gentle whispers that the heart of the Light Warrior continues to pulse. Michael's battle with Lucifer (Prince of Darkness) demonstrates that a pure spirit can fight and defeat the most evil of opponents. **Archangel Michael is a powerful Master of Light. He is the Dragon Slayer, warrior spirit of God, whisper in my ear, friend and constant companion.** It is because of Michael this knowledge will continue.

Possessing a hallowed cause easily justifies a move into action; however, this battle should be waged within before true purpose can be found. The Code of the Third Millennium Warrior instructs that a true warrior emerges as a warrior of self first. They must stand willing to fight the good fight on a daily basis to live and represent a virtuous life. Teach no warrior to move into action before he or she has faced the enemies within. As you succeed in facing, exposing and defeating your fear-based negativity, the true purpose of your existence becomes clearer. Fear keeps much of your purpose hidden until your quest for Truth can no longer be contained. If you have ever asked the question, *"Who am I and why am I here"* then you have taken the first step by asking the Correct Question. This is an example of the Human Being searching to remember the lost knowledge of what it is like being Human. This question rocks the foundation of Darkness because it challenges the level of Truth in which you exist. The power of the Correct Question has immense transformational repercussions. This is why it can take so long to build up the courage to ask it. Sometimes years of effort will only bring forward the success of asking the Correct Question. **If you do not ask the Higher Self questions then the Higher Self assumes the Lower Self knows.** The Higher Self sees the Lower through the eyes of perfection and therefore assumes you have all that you need. When you become lost, tell your higher spiritual guidance that you're lost. Help will be dispatched your way. Pay attention because how you receive your guidance can come in any shape or circumstance. It is important to recognize the value of the request. The Correct Question is a true victory. Natural progression is to seek out answers. This will extend the student-teacher classroom into a broader expansion of your Universe. It will be then that the Masters of Light can easily teach those that listen. Everything you need for victory has been supplied, but it is up to you to find it. There are no mistakes, only tests and lessons. Granted some lessons seem like punishment, but misery ends when you fully gain the value of the lesson. You must understand that victory may be different from your expectations. Here are examples: You may seek wealth and find charity, or seek truth to find love or you may seek love and find yourself.

Probing for the Correct Question is based on the notion that nothing concerning the human body is just physical. There are emotions that support our conditions as well as ideas that support our emotions. The mind's stream of consciousness is an amazingly complex issue and many times the body is the last phase of the process. In most cases the body will create a condition simply to wake us up to issues we are not dealing with. For example: A woman may over eat to obesity and unhappiness because she fears facing what her beauty and sexuality may attract. Thus, dieting never works because the original issue of fear was never exposed. Therefore the Correct Question was never asked. Here is a hypothetical situation with this imagined woman.

Q) Why do you eat?
A) I like food.
Q) Why do you like food?
A) Because, I enjoy it, it makes me feel good.
Q) What is it that makes you feel good?
A) It is the pleasure of satisfying my desires.
Q) Then why are you unhappy?
A) Because I am fat and unattractive.

CQ) *How does being unattractive satisfy your desires?*

Here we can begin with the Correct Question to find the real truth.

Magic and miracles are rich for the seeker on a journey. Miracles are wondrous things but if they are difficult to see, a blockage of memory has occurred. Faith is paramount for a miracle walker. If the knowledge isn't immediately clear, we must believe that somewhere, someone or something exists with the knowledge we need. **Seek out the knowledge.** It is either within you or around you. The more answers, the easier the process. In many cases, the process itself can have more value than the accomplishment, which explains why we take on another project immediately after attaining our most recent goals. What we learn along the way reminds us of our warrior potential, which reminds us of *"Who we are and why we are here."* Human beings are the only creatures on this planet that has forgotten who they are. We have forgotten the heart of what it means being human. Sometimes the sum of our experience leads us directly into uncertainty. When in doubt of the solution, search for the question that can illustrate the story and possibly offer the missing piece. For example:

What do I need? What does happiness look like? What's the next step? What's the block? How do I improve? What's the lesson? What's the wrong thing to do? What is victory?

These are just a few Correct Questions that can launch the seeker on a journey. From asking the question a new adventure for knowledge and purpose begins. **The Discipline necessary to pursue the Truth is the Second Challenge of the Light Warrior.**

LESSON ELEVEN

Winds of Change

In every life comes a time when our internal and external maturity creates a change in our identity. Maturity is a transformational process. It takes us from what we once were to what we must be. The old way of life (or the way of life that is no longer relevant) must die away to live again as new. This idea of alchemy is as old as time. Transformation from death to rebirth must occur in order for life to continue. This will happen individually and globally. The Culture of the Forgotten Truth programs you to believe that death is an un-Godly and horrible reality. The concept of "The Happy Ending" has been perpetuated and re-enacted on such a grand scale that the natural passing from one life to another is met with contempt and disbelief. However, death is all around us, but then, so is life. The two are intertwined in the ongoing five stages of rebirth: **1) Death, 2) Decay, 3) Fertilization, 4) Gestation,** and **5) Rebirth**. With death the journey continues uninterrupted. Mourn it, honor it, accept it, and then rejoice in the new life to come. This is the way of all natural things. We have all experienced some sort of dying but may not have recognized it. It is when the "what once was" and the "what can no longer be" dies away so that you can ascend into your new way of life. This simply means that your life has changed forever and there is no going back. Only then can the son become a man or the daughter become a woman. The passing of innocence into maturity is normally perceived, like the birthing of children, as a painful process, but does not always have to be. Shape shifting is a natural skill that can be developed with practice. The elements necessary to shift shape require desire and a totally complete understanding of the image into which you wish to shift your shape. You must know what you want in order to

become it. The Culture of the Forgotten Truth encourages you
to box yourself in rooms away from nature, thus keeping nature
on the other side of walls while you stare hypnotically at
propaganda devices. This detaches us from nature and seduces
away our shape shifting birthrights. We are left mindlessly
changing channels, hoping to find some sense of fulfillment.
These hypnotic devices perpetuate the fallacy that nature can
be controlled and that normally all stories conclude with a
"Happy Ending." This is not to say that happiness cannot be
found in the rebirth process; however, **"At the end of life there
will be death."** Rebirth waits on the other side of the dying
process and the faster you learn this, the easier you can move
gracefully through the five stages. To conclude a loving
relationship, for example, is a death-to-rebirth process. First,
the relationship ends (Death). You then suffer the loss (Decay).
Next you force yourself to make new relationships with others,
with yourself or with your higher spiritual power (Fertilization).
You then nurture these relationships (Gestation) and eventually
you come out of it with an improved relationship with yourself
or you meet someone else (Rebirth). A change in vocation,
moving from student to teacher, and countless other
transformations define this rebirth process. Please understand:
the process of life to death is designed to teach us the very
things we need to learn. In time we must all accept that death
balances life, especially if you've chosen a warrior's path.
Maturing beyond outdated patterns into wisdom is a graceful
rebirth. **We all reach a point when the person we are now is
no longer the person we once were.** This is looking at the
carnage and devastation of your past, knowing full well that
you can never go back. You then have conquered the past
Dragons and are ready to move forward in your quest for life's
rewards. You have stepped into your power by traveling through
the process of death to rebirth and you have shape shifted. The
mature self is then blessed with veteran experience and can
teach the lessons learned to others. The Natural Law of Maturity
is difficult, but the process can move faster if you surrender

and gracefully accept that this is nature's way. It is written in the Tao Te Ching, "Nature does not have a human heart." The human heart is a powerful gift from God, but sometimes we use it against ourselves and give the dying process emotional power over us. Growth is the purpose for the Laws of Maturity and knowing that this natural law exists can give you a sense of security in that there is life after death. However, it is also equally natural to grieve. Growing out of pain is a part of who we are. **The Acceptance of Truth (Patience by means of Surrender) is the Third Challenge of the Light Warrior.**

LESSON TWELVE

Fear of Commitment

A Winged Dragon

The word "Commitment" had lost much of its appeal by the end of the Twentieth century. Committing to a choice requires a warrior's heart and thus dedication to an end result. Most people perceive commitment as work. If so, they are correct at least in the beginning. Commitment is an Ancient Art of Discipline and is what we must develop in our quest to live a warrior's life. Commitment, like all Martial Arts, improves with practice. Without commitment, we open ourselves to the perpetual seduction of indecision. This is simply hesitation, and hesitation can develop into stagnation. Commitment is necessary to attain victory because without it your life would have little challenge. The loss of commitment in today's generations has brought rise to a defeatist mentality. Noncommittal relationships are accepted to pacify the fear of making a mistake. A lack of commitment to honesty leads to dissension and loss of dependability. As a result trust will falter, and without trust, all relationships lose their footing. This is not to say that there is no hope after trust is damaged; however, commitment to the truth is the only hope for restoring trust.

This manuscript offers truth and reflects honesty; but now we have reached a place of conviction. To fully embrace The Code of The Third Millennium Warrior requires a commitment. However, this commitment is to no one but you. Ultimately, you will judge yourself by the commitments you made and completed. Pacifism and lack of commitment have created a programmed virus for the Twentieth century. **Pacifism is the Art of Doing Nothing.** Your time to prove your warrior status has come. Warrior's of Light must face their convictions and live an example of truth, courage and compassion. With this commitment in your heart, you will strengthen even a shaky stance. If you already have a solid foothold this commitment will provide an even stronger foundation. Through conviction, the power of your heart will soar to new levels of elevation. Imagine a clean, new start without judgment, shame or the fear of commitment.

Fear of Commitment is the belief that the unimportant takes precedence over the real. The real is living Truth, Light and Love. Your discipline in the journey of Love and Light is as real as your applied effort. Without this determination, one would not show up to achieve. We all have a fight or flight mechanism. The fear of commitment is a winged fear creating a desire to fly away. This winged Dragon would never allow you to focus on finishing what you've started, thus whisking you from one unfinished thing to another. However, this time you have a guide to help you overcome your seductions. The Code of The Third Millennium Warrior is designed to empower you so that you can complete your mission. It was written for this and requires nothing less. Do not be afraid to commit to a relationship with your greater self based on honesty and trust. Do not be afraid to commit to a better way of life. Stabilize your stance and stabilize your fears. You may even have what it takes to be a guiding light for humanity if you can commit to being so. A clean, pure heart is the strongest weapon in the universe when combating evil. No Lord of Darkness has reign in the Kingdom of Light. We possess the key to that power and to the unified awakening here on earth. Take from the Light; it is here for you. Take as much as you feel you deserve and then take ten thousand times more. You cannot exhaust its supply. Darkness only has the power that you give it and a commitment to the Light will expose the delusions that sidetrack a warrior on a mission. Look at what is real and unreal. Your illusions of selfishness are based on fear and lies. You already know this and yet you still hesitate. Why? Are you afraid you will make a mistake? If so, ask yourself, "Can I work with my present situations or not?" Make a choice and then concern yourself with the issue of conviction. What you stand for is who you are and how you will be remembered. How many times over and over have you learned this lesson? Trust in yourself and in your Truth, and then fight for what your heart determines is real. Visualize the image of who you want to be and commit to it. Make this moment complete. **Commit to a greater concept of you.** To become a Defender of Light is a commitment. You live in a great time with the potential for great Light if you can make a stand and commit to your own greatness.

LESSON THIRTEEN

The Dragon's Lair

Through an entryway, down a corridor exists a chamber into the darkest of places. Within this chamber dwells a sleeping horror resting silently in its lair. This is the dark door of fear itself. Occasionally we will venture to such a place, and occasionally images of fear will venture out from such a place. These fear-based images of ruin seem to exist, but from where? The better question may be, "How can fear be exposed?" Where is your deepest fear and how do you find the Dragon's Lair? The answer is simple if you can grasp that the Dragon is pure manifestation, or MAN-infestation. God did not create the Dragon because the Dragon is an illusion. This is why you cannot find him under the bed. Dragons exist in shadows where light is blocked. It is a thought-created entity and you must look inward to recognize its outward mutations. In the dark-side of your imagination the Dragons dwell. You have the power to access your own evil as well as the ability to access the clarity to manifest evil's destruction. In short, **you are the Dragon's Lair**. You are the vessel and the creator of all that you fear. God did not create fear, you did. God did, however, grant you the power to create your dreams. Fear is God's light blocked. When tempted, fear roams among the images of your mind until it can find a gateway to attach itself to the physical world. It is up to you to recognize that you have equal power to create and destroy. Only with this understanding can you proceed on the warrior's path to overcome your darkness. It takes discipline to sustain virtue and it is virtue that slays the Dragon.

In a world filled with trouble, worry, debt and dissension, there is little time to indulge in the fantasies of Dragons. Dragons, however, are a compelling concept because in almost every culture there is some historical belief in this mystical and mythical icon. Some cultures see Dragons as a symbol of power and some as a symbol of darkness, and without doubt Darkness does have its power. Nonetheless, there is no physical proof they have ever existed. So why do the fantasy and lore live on? The story of their power continues in legend, myth or prophecy. This supports a belief that if they don't exist then they once must have. Imagine for a moment there is a realm where they do exist. From their realm to ours they would be able to shape shift. Shape shifting is the key to understanding the Dragon, moreover the key to reversing their power. Transform fear by exercising courage. Surrender yourself to the possibility of victory. Surrender to truth and conquer a lie. Question first pre-taught, fear-based propaganda and try a different way. If you try, then you have taken another step toward freedom. Hunt the Dragon down and face fear with extreme intent. The Code of the Third Millennium Warrior can help you understand the magic power of your Dragons. The Dragon Slayer is a resurrection of warrior spirit. Tao of the Dragon Slayer is the seeker, pathfinder, hunter, achiever, and above all, the warrior. Like the caterpillar that transforms into a beautiful butterfly, the Dragon Slayer is the heart of a warrior that can transform into a warrior of the heart. You must eventually face your Dragons if you wish to continue evolving on your journey for truth. You must find the courage to venture into the Dragon's lair.

Imagination is a seed of memory. It's more vivid as a child, but we tend to set childlike ideas aside as we grow older. Imagine for a moment another place where life is blissful. A paradise of wonder where you are strong, feel joy and love life. This is your paradise, it's the "wouldn't life be great if . . ." place. We can all imagine a place of total comfort. In our comforting place there is a master, the ruler, the leader, the warrior of that reality. This warrior is you. It is the inner you, the voice and Master in your heart, the strong you that you wish to be. The warrior spirit is your image of power, in control and without fear. From this picture we have the inner you living in a place of wonder, existing only to enjoy life. Your "Place of Power" is as good a name as any. Playing creatively like a child is recommended to remember childlike memories of this place. In your Place of Power things are the way life should be, except for one detail. There are Dark negative forces, creatures that can roam in this world. These creatures are of the utmost relevance because they have a talent for shape shifting into your darkest torments. **Dragons tap into your thoughts and manifest as your fears, seductions or addictions.** When one of these torments appears, it ascends on this Place of Power. Paradise then begins to change. (Nothing of course has really changed, but you suddenly become stressed with life for the moment.) Now your focus is not on the love of life but on fear and negativity, blame and resentment. The warrior's strength **turns** against itself and the battle creates a destructive inner conflict. Your Place of Power is in danger and you must face a decision. Will I accept this fear in my world and find a way to coexist with the stress, or will I slay the vile thing and expose it for what it truly is? To suffer or to fight is an old question.

*"To be or not to be? That is the question. Whether it is nobler to **suffer** the slings and arrows of outrageous fortune or **take arms against** a sea of troubles thus opposing them to die or sleep." William Shakespeare*

Christian prophecy in the Book of Revelations foretells of a Red Dragon with seven heads that will come and orchestrate massive inhumanities leading to a great war. The battle of Light and Dark begins with the soul.

It is an unenviable task **to define**, and also to convince you that there are Dragons roaming. Please continue to remain open to the infinite possibilities that exist with shape shifting, alternate realities, dimensional gateways, myths and legends. The information that follows may or may not test your imagination, but it will challenge your system of practical thinking. Whatever reasons you have to dismiss fantasy, this must be understood: **not all "fantasy" is fantasy.** Yesterday's fiction is becoming today's reality. There are parallel realities that overlap each other constantly. Dragons have been a grand metaphor for centuries; this much is not hard to accept. But their existence may be harder to swallow. How Dragons roam is as mysterious as the power of the Dragon itself. The Dragon's lair exists in a

Dimension of Thought and in your power to manifest on a negative level. The power you have to delve into mystical ways is greater than you know. Your life to date is determined with your power to manifest. If mankind was created in the image of the Creator, then doesn't this mean that Man was created to create? Dragons in their imagined form exist only in a nonphysical reality or we would have found a fossil by now. Alternate realities have gateways unlocked by your thoughts. Have you ever been afraid of something that was never there? Is a reality real if it's in your head? It's an extraordinary coincidence that so many different people and so many different cultures have the same reality of a Dragon. It's the recurring coincidences that suggest its validity. Can Dragons simply transform? Are we so practical that we must see to believe? It is the essence of fear that creates fear. "All we have to fear is fear itself." Do we not just attach the essence of fear to a thing we can see? Dragons are masters at deception by blocking clarity. The dragons of seduction are the ones we welcome most. As I have stated, there are **The Nine Spiritual Seductions of Darkness**. Each can be balanced only with virtue.

Seduction	*Virtue*
1. **Anger**	*Forgiveness, Compassion, Mercy*
2. **Pride**	*Humility*
3. **Deceit**	*Honesty*
4. **Envy**	*Respect, Gratitude, Joy*
5. **Greed**	*Compassion, Generosity, Selfless*
6. **Fear**	*Courage*
7. **Gluttony**	*Patience, Discipline, Sobriety*
8. **Lust**	*Honor*
9. **Sloth**	*Faith, Action*

Seductions can overlap each other. Virtues also overlap to combat weakness. If all nine seductions win the soul, pure Evil is unleashed against humanity. If all nine virtues are attained a

guide or prophet for humanity emerges. The false prophet may have some virtue but fall short of all of them. You are no stranger to these seductions, and they are not strangers to you. You have already allowed at least one of these seductions to dominate temptation throughout your life. Recognize and reflect that you have fallen prey in at least one of these nine categories of seduction. All of us have. One of these Dragons is closer to you than the others. Take a moment and reflect upon the behavior pattern that you have struggled with time and again. Consider your life story with clear honesty. These seductions block your Light, which creates a false illusion that you are separated from your God source. These behavior patterns thrive in an unhealthy state and have taunted your soul with poor choices. If you allow this internal battle for your soul to wage unchecked then you may find yourself alone against an unbeatable addiction. **You must want this fight to win it.** Your seductions have caused you stagnation and there is no more time to waste. "The crusades live again, but this time in reverse."
Tao of the Dragon Slayer

LESSON FOURTEEN

Be the Truth or Be the Lie

The Water Dragon

It can be a cold awakening to realize that you are what you say every time you say it. So much of our reality is a reflection of words. If what you say is false, then you live with a false image. If you speak from the heart you can reflect true sincerity. Although you may not realize it completely, you stand alone in your perception of yourself. You have a unique essence of self that gives you individuality, and no one can take that. However, you can give it away and along with it your power. Your individuality is what makes you special. Your self-image is a reflection of so many realities creating who you are. The God-gift of individuality is the package from which the gift of free-will is delivered. **Individuality is your interpretation of free-will**. If your self-image is less than unique, then you have lost a rich quality of life. It's imperative that you claim your God-gifts. This quest must be internal with little concern for outside opinions. The "I am" is the ego and each of us must determine how we wish to shape ourselves. Do not become sidetracked by blaming people who you believe stole your identity. It is more important to learn wisdom from the experience. Chasing the past can only postpone the quality of your future. If your parents were not what you intended, try to see them in a different light. Focus on their highest Light and you may find that it remotely resembles some qualities of your highest Light. All things happen for a reason, your parents included. If you focus on their darkest traits, then you may only continue to welcome their Darkness into your heart. There is a reason this relationship was formed. If nothing else, a veteran's experience on the battlefield, no matter how horrid, can be priceless in terms of wisdom. If there is no apparent clue why you have the parents you have, then herein reveals a quest for Truth. A quest for Truth begins with a question, then faith and movement. In the end, all Truths will be realized. The sooner this is accepted the faster you can grow through it. To achieve success while questing for Truth you must first personify honesty to find honesty. The words you choose affect who you are and of what you are capable. "As above so then below," every truth and every lie you speak affect you internally and externally. It is naive to believe that just because someone didn't react immediately to a lie that they were deceived. Most people know immediately when they are being lied to but would rather choose not to confront the liar. As it is supposed to be, the liar inevitably deceives him or herself. The liar after all is the one trying to make sense out of deception. The liar does not believe that a lie is harmful. The liar has delusions believing that the lie is doing a good thing, maybe helping in some false way. The liar lives in a world of untruths, and so what is real becomes illusive. Living in the non-real is what will always destroy the liar. Unless the liar changes, defeat is always the liar's end. Unfortunately, it may not happen in your preferred time frame. If the liar is strong it can take a while, but you can speed up the process by reflecting the Truth to combat the liar. If you reflect Light, as the liar reflects Darkness, eventually the Dragon will be exposed. The Water Dragon is a shadowy reflection. It is slippery and changes image to suit our desires never completely taking an honest form. These tricks are nothing but illusions and manifest only a temporary projection. Lies can hide the Truth, mask it, try to distort it, and even manipulate it, but the Truth always remains the Truth. The Truth is constant in the scheme of Universal Law. Your intentions when allied with your highest Truth can merge with Universal Truth. This is a great achievement. Otherwise, if you do not speak out the voice of Truth it becomes stuck in the throat and creates illness. Speaking your honesty is the beginning of a much broader picture. It is living and being the Truth that possesses the grandest Light.

Speaking the words and living the words differentiate religion and spirituality. The words of religion are the vehicle for the spiritual experience. Words and experience are a divine matrimony. Transformation of this magnitude does not happen overnight, but in time people will look to you for honesty. You will come to understand why your opinion has value and realize your own value. When you reflect honestly you encounter Truth. The merger of your Truth with Universal Truth will create a beacon of Light throughout the cosmos. Merge with the Universe is how the Warrior slays the Dragons of illusion.

LESSON FIFTEEN

The Art of Sabotage

The victimized soul is the most common image of social breakdown in the era of modern Man. This image has reached widespread appeal in the scientific age to the point of becoming a philosophy. Granted, everyone has been the target of attack at some point in their lives and some Dark memories remain for a lifetime. The focus here is not on a victim of crime or a victim of circumstance, but instead on the person who thrives on the energy of victimization. The victimization persona is a selfish desire to feed off of someone's positive polarity using a negative polarity with a strategy of sorrow and/ or persecution. In an age of self-help Gurus and expensive therapy, the Code of Third Millennium Warrior requires that you stand and fight. It's been said, "Misery loves company," and while this may be true, the company most assuredly does not love misery. One must recognize his or her own self-absorption and how destructive it is to people around you. If not, then the victim becomes the victimizer. Self-absorption means to dwell an illusion to death. This is counter-productive and should be recognized as weak. Always combat an internal weakness with a strategy. Write your strategy down to make it real. If there is no apparent strategy, then seek out knowledge to form a strategy. From a healthier outlook you will always remember the time you "picked yourself up" and got yourself better. This memory brings strength, and that is the way it works. The victim should not depend on others to make them better because that too is avoiding the problem. The victimized martyr is an image based on a sacrificial delusion. Victimized martyrs are rarely asked to martyr themselves because they do it freely. Do not give in to their claims of necessary self-destruction. Drama sets the stage for the Art of Sabotage.

It's the empowerment of the Warrior Spirit that is required to overcome victimization and it is the act of self-ability that is always remembered as the torch that lit the flame. Victims are experts at finding people to be sympathetic. Sympathy serves to a degree but action and love is necessary to complete the healing. The habitual offender of victimization has a vampire effect on people's energy. The requirements to fulfill such neediness can drain the life out of even the most powerful person. **Victimization is an addiction that creates sabotage to dramatize the victim's needs.** Most people tend to sabotage to some degree anyway rather than face their full potential. Sabotage is the most widely used tactic to avoid one's fears and withdraw back into a more familiar situation. Some people will sabotage a relationship at the point of getting close (fear of commitment or change). Some people ruin a job at the time when success is at their fingertips (fear of success, change or even greatness). Some people sabotage their health so not to face life itself. These are just a few examples of how sabotage works. In most cases we don't even know we are doing it until it's too late. Victimization is a virus program that can remain dormant until your resistance is low. It takes persistent introspection to recognize the patterns of self-destruction. Correcting the behavior is the next step. Viewing your life story and logging the tragedy is one method. **This is effective as long as the emotions are not relived.** Attaching the emotion only serves as a punishment for experiences long passed. View yourself through the eyes of clarity, not the eyes of shame. Try to use this affirmation when things seem hopeless: **"It is what it is, and nothing more."** Detach the blame and emotional persecution. **Blame is just a conversation that defines failure.** There are no mistakes, only tests and lessons. If you have a need to blame yourself, then plan and **write down** an appropriate atonement, serve that goal, forgive yourself, and move on. Understand, however, this is only an exercise of your own personal condemnation and judgmental desires. The Army of Light will not wait on those who dwell too long in their shadow and self-pity. The time is now to rise above the past and take hold of your destiny. If misfortune continually keeps you in a place of stagnation, then possibly you are unconsciously afraid. Face the fear, break free and do battle with the Dragons that make you weak. Do not be ashamed of fear. It is a worthy enemy sent here to teach you about courage. There is no need to martyr or suffer any longer. Fear is the Dragon, it is the enemy, and an enemy always should be respected. However, **even the demons of hell have no choice but to stand down in the face of a passionate warrior on a rampage to victory. Be That Warrior.**

LESSON SIXTEEN

Dying Ground

Shock Treatment for the Soul

On the other side of despair there is an image of clarity that stands between the past and the future. It is life and death, heaven and hell. It is the clarity of nonlinear reality. It is clear and present danger. Hopelessness can deliver a gift called Dying Ground. Most of us choose to exist from one perception to another, seeing what is **true enough.** Deep Truth requires sensitivity, commitment and honesty. The pursuit of deep Truth should be considered a path similar to a Martial Artist's because "The Truth can kick your ass." Because the hard Truth can be devastating, it is important to realize that a moment of truth is a force with which to reckon. It is important in times of great need to recognize that life sometimes places us on "Dying Ground" where everyday we wake up in the morning and must fight to win the day. In these difficult times, every choice needs to be a good one. How will you stand when this moment affects forever? How will you live or how will you die? Inevitably, life and death will represent each other. Could you change a pattern or habit that has little value in the fulfillment of your soul's destiny? Patterns occur when a system of belief manifests into a reality. These patterns serve a purpose, and then fade into the abyss. A pattern that no longer serves your Truth will only cause stagnation. This stagnation has no objective in the living and expanding universe. All living things are in motion no matter what delays we may attempt. In time, the universe will force change, sometimes violently. **Shock treatment for the soul** is what happens with this type of violent change. Shock is an effective method by which to break old patterns. Some even wait until the universe does the inevitable, relying on outside factors to save them from "rock bottom." Do not make the mistake of ignoring the laws of motion. If you prefer pacifism to passion, then you may be stagnated. Being passive during impending consequences can sometimes create unfavorable outcomes. If denial of this Truth exists, then be prepared to accept what is coming. Refusing to deal honestly with an issue is the strategy of futility. We must have faith, "In the end all Truths will be realized." Dying Ground is where your past, present and future meet on a battlefield. It is the point where survival kicks in and nothing else matters. It is the realization of how your poor choices have all culminated in a moment of Truth. Dying Ground is when you realize that you represent either a living or a dying reality. Will you fight for the love of life, or will you lie down for the Creatures of Darkness to devour? In most cases it is addiction that reveals Dying Ground. **An addiction is a weakness that occurs when the warrior spirit is lost or forgotten.** *Addiction is the opposite of Warrior spirit.* A moment of clarity can present itself just before the moment of no return. Many people do not survive this moment. Some souls are just too far lost, but even for the lost soul there is a hope. If you have misused your God-gifts, then Dying Ground may be your last chance for salvation. Dying Ground is to be respected. It can kick in the fight or flight instincts that awaken the Dragon Slayer. **Many people simply forget that they know how to fight.** A reminder of this ability is a blessing. Do not take it lightly and do not allow this kind of clarity to slip away in the sludge of previous ideas. After all, it's our previous poor judgments that deliver us to present problems. You may need to conquer or surrender to the winds of change. As long as you have choices you are still in the game. **Defeat is to lose your ability to choose.** Defeat is unacceptable to a warrior. God has given you free-will, with it comes the right to fight. Cherish this gift because it is a divine link between you and God. Even on the battlefield, surrounded by Darkness, Light can shine if you remain connected to your God source. Give practice to seeing a visual link from heaven to the top of your head. This is the crown of royalty. In difficult situations, remind yourself to know your enemy and your true royal-self. You may find they are not far from being the same, yet the Truth will remove the blocks and expose the fear and weaknesses. Expose your weakness and you will empower your life with purpose. **Overcoming our unhealthy behavior is *The Tao of the Dragon Slayer.*** We only recognize the evils of Darkness by what we understand most about ourselves.

LESSON SEVENTEEN

Shape Shifting

Shape Shifting is a concept-to-concept exchange. It's simpler than you may be aware. We all have the ability to shape shift energy. We change our emotions, our ideas, our moods and our body on a regular basis. We may change our body to reshape our emotions or motivate our emotions to reshape our body. We may wake up tired, take a shower, have some coffee, and burst out the door ready to take on a brand new day. Moving from tired to excited may not seem like our ancient concept of Shape Shifting but in fact it is. There are only two skills required to energetically shift one's shape.

1st. *You must be able to completely let go of the concept and rigidity of your present form.* (Surrender the "I Am")

2nd. *You must be able to fully comprehend the form in which you are taking.* (Conquer the "I Am now")

Before one can become advanced in Shape Shifting, both skills must be refined. To develop either of these skills to higher levels you must first accept that form is energy and that our form is a product of how we have focused our energy. Our thoughts, our emotions and our actions combined create this concept of who we are. In the beginning certain ideas must be accepted on faith. Seeing yourself as a concept, for example, will take time and effort. The concept of "you" has been generated, nurtured and reinforced. Your parents started this concept, and then your environment, teachers, lessons, tests, experiences and cultural protocol nurtured and reinforced it. A programming effect begins at infancy and is perpetuated throughout your life. You are bred to be who you are. The level of greatness to which you take this concept is up to your awareness and dedication.

Our ancestors learned how to shape shift with the animals and nature. Animal Shape Shifting is the most recognized idea of this ancient shamanic art form. However, the second requirement of Shape Shifting indicates, *"You must be able to fully comprehend the form in which you are taking."* Modern mankind would find this difficult considering how we have separated ourselves from animals and nature. We are far more concerned with domesticating animals to be obedient than learning their consciousness. However, gender Shape Shifting is widely embraced. The skill to change form is as common as changing your clothes to feel better or taking a bath to feel refreshed. It's simple on a basic scale and powerful on an advanced level. Shape Shifting oneself can heal the pain of one's present circumstance. This can be swift or it may take years to release rigid concepts. What is important is that you have the faith that it can be done. Faith is what transforms a basic skill into a higher spiritual endowment. If you believe you are . . . then you will become. The "I think, therefore, I am" idea, is a beautiful beginning; however, the emotional, the physical and the spiritual realms can also be developed to support one's altered shaping. In many cases shape shifting is used for natural healing as in shifting from a painful body to a pain free body. Shape shifting one's own spine is a good place to correct posture and develop higher body potential. Shifting the hips is excellent for developing freedom and grace through movement and flexibility. When the hips are free we release much of our rigidity. Hip flexibility training can offer a good place for the beginning Shape Shifter to develop exercises to free their body. The mind and the heart must practice flexibility training as well.

Energy transformation is a universal opportunity, and we are not alone in our ability to draw upon it. Dimensional shifting is as common as shifting your mood. Shifting is occurring whether you are aware of it or not. Internal conflict, for example, could be two opposing concepts trying to shift into form. A common illustration of this might be a moral program and sexual fantasy both trying to manifest. The opposing intention creates the conflict as an internal dimensional battle. Any battle that takes place in a nonphysical realm, will undoubtedly transform your world from one dimension to another. Dimensional shifts are how the dragons of fear, seduction and addiction emerge to take shape from other realms into your physical world. We are motivated by two primary instincts, fear and pleasure. For the most part people in general attach fear to conflict and battle. The dragon shifts into the image of something stressful. The conflict then promotes your fear, and the dragons feed off the energy of fear which shifts you into a stressful person. The same goes for seduction and addiction. The dragons block your clarity; shift into your seduction, manifest an illusion that seduces you off your path. This is a proven strategy of Darkness and your participation is the fuel that feeds it. Negativity will feed the negative. You have a gift to shape shift and you are being called to use it. The direction toward the positive or the negative is up to you. You may believe you have little control over fear; this is because fear blocks your Light. Combat the Dragons of fear and seduction by Shape Shifting into the Warrior. Only two things are necessary to shape shift into the Warrior. You must let go of the victim and you must recognize a new concept with a stronger self-image. Tao of the Dragon Slayer is a chosen path to shift anger to forgiveness, pride to humility, deceit to honesty, envy to gratitude, greed to generosity, fear to courage, lust to honor, and laziness to action. It's not as important that we all learn how to shift from a human being into an animal. It is important we learn to shift from a human being into a more evolved human being. Possibly, as better human beings we will know respect for our animal brothers and sisters. Hopefully as we evolve, we will learn to respect ourselves. From the beginning of time we have always had a constant choice, develop higher or stay the same. It's an inbred instinct for the human race to evolve. You can deny your part in this evolution, but you cannot deny a history of exploration and development. It may seem you are alone, but this is a shallow Truth. The deeper Truth is that you are a part of a highly sophisticated network of beings that are shifting into a united consciousness. Union and peace is the future. You may wish to keep things the same, but time will force changes. You will excel if you can develop skills that allow you to shift and move quickly through changes and develop yourself to shift into a more empowered state. Whether student is shifting into teacher or teacher into master, you have more conscious ability than you know. Be aware that with practice and dedication you can change to become the victory you seek. It is not easy work. You will need your warrior power to give you strength. Embrace the concept of warrior masters. Take a step forward from who you are to who you should be. The warrior in you is waiting for you.

LESSON EIGHTEEN

Seeds of Memory

Much documentation has been written describing human behavior. We have a story unlike any species that lives on this planet. We are different and do not know why. Why is the human race different? From the beginning of time, an animal such as a deer has survived through the day and rested at nightfall. For thousands of years animals of this type have continued to do so unchanged. The ancestors of the other creatures that inhabit this planet are also barely evolving, except for one. There is only one creature of this planet that is dramatically driven: driven to excel, grow, learn and evolve on its own. Unlike other creatures we are even driven to destroy ourselves. Only one creature appears unique among the billions of other creatures living in harmony with this planet. Ironically, we are the one creature that has the most difficulty finding harmony with the nature of our planet. The human being is in many ways the most alien creature to earth. We are the one species on earth that's forgotten who we are, why we are here and what we are supposed to do. Most people cannot even figure out what will make them content. A squirrel knows how to be a squirrel and is content to be a squirrel. It goes through its day happy to be what it is, but human beings for the most part, are not. Why are we discontent? Why do we need to develop and grow and reach further, go faster, expand beyond previous limitations, and what is it that we intend on achieving with all this effort? What would bring us satisfaction? Where is the source of this information? Did we journey from heaven to be here? Are we from the stars? Within every individual there is memory locked and stored away for only the most introspective to reveal. Most people do not even realize that their actions are based on fulfilling a purpose that was planted deep inside their being long ago. **"Real knowledge is not learned but instead remembered"**. So then what is it that we are remembering? The answers are all around you and are far more simple than you think. As students we are here to document all experiences with Words. The words create languages, the languages create common ways and the understanding of each other's language is growing. A collective consciousness or united body of knowledge is and has always been our burning, driving memory. From the beginning of time people have been trying to link consciousness with something outside or beyond one's self. Unfortunately, most people have had difficulty grasping an etheric concept of collective consciousness. Our history gives us names of a chosen few such as Jesus, Buddha, or Mohammed and so on that have broken through the Gateway to achieve enlightenment. Everyone else continues to use what they know to be effective such as our ideas, emotions and our hands. The last piece to the collective puzzle goes beyond our mental, emotional and physical concepts. Modern mankind continues to develop ideas that link communication through space and all around the world. We have developed intelligence systems that link us to all points of the globe, and we have audio/visual devices to transport images and sounds to almost every person's home on the planet. What modern technology has accomplished to link one person to another is staggering. One need only ask, "Why is it so necessary that mankind be driven to communicate?" Could it be a seed of memory (existing program)? We all possess this seed to unite and become whole. It is a burning desire in our evolution and we must not allow fear to hinder or block the process. Our history reveals union is evolution. Man unites with woman and creates a new generation. Even our wars inevitably merge cultures. "The Gateway has opened" and it is time for the next phase of evolution. A leap of faith offers us the ability to accept that we have moved beyond mind and body limitations. We must realize that a spiritual unity is our next phase of growth: A Union of Light, developed and nurtured, one by one. This is the hope of the ancient Masters and our continued true purpose. Our Ancient memory is the soul's intention and centuries of purpose. Light and vibration are what link us to each other, to ourselves, to nature and to the divine. Singing illustrates this concept as great masses of people can harmonize to one voice and one vibration. Accept the call and relive with us the memories that unite us. If you can see through childish indifference and form a deliberate understanding of unlocked memory, maybe then working together we can complete the Circle of Light. Maybe then we will remember why we are here. Maybe then we can return to the heavens.

LESSON NINETEEN

Dimension of Thought

You are a concept. The entire reality of who you are exists in your thoughts. "I think, therefore I am" *(Descartes)*. The more focused your thoughts, the more powerful. The more positive you think, the more positive your power becomes; likewise the more worrisome your thoughts, the more negatively powerful you become. To fully understand oneself as a concept takes years of research and evaluation. It is you studying who you are. It is important to know your strengths and weaknesses. Knowing who you are is crucial to having a powerful self-presence. It's been said, "If you do not tell people who you are, then they will tell you who you are." Words are vessels that transport vibration from one Dimension to another. These vessels resurrect as information in a Dimension of Thought, and then are carried across your reality. The Dimension of Thought exists in a concept. The concept is memory and imagination, which pits the real against the unreal for supremacy. Internal chatter or the judgmental inner critic wages conflict in our minds, our hearts, and in our everyday actions. The Judgmental concept we have of ourselves creates a rigid version of who we are. It is sometimes difficult to break free from our concepts of whom we are; yet this is how to dispel old negative patterns. The illusion of the unreal generates a massive arsenal of ignorance, which assaults and insults what is Love. Loving the very thing that bothers you about yourself can heal the negative mind. Your negative motivated arsenal uses the Word to transport the unclean thoughts to block your compassionate soul, but the compassionate soul by definition projects Light. Honesty and courage create a defense against ignorance and fear, which helps to let go of old out-dated images. Do not become lost in trivial negative belief patterns. Negative belief patterns can sometimes reach a chronic level such as obsessive-compulsive behavior. Negative judgment can lead to depression. A block that overshadows your compassionate loving self causes both of these conditions. It is important to realize the negative can overrun the self if the positive does not neutralize the imbalance. Obsessive-compulsive behavior is energy charged to create conflict. This conflict is based on negative friction. To attack conflict with more negative conflict only supports and feeds the negative imbalance. Depression and obsession can be neutralized by a loving defense reflected back on to the inner judgment that is attacking. Meet critical judgment and obsession with compassion and kindness by setting up a beloved dialogue with your critical self. You may find the kindness rises to a moral high ground above the critic and the inner chatter diminishes. Depression can also be neutralized by a loving dialogue with the self. Meet this with maturity and gratitude, because even the tough criticism has an ulterior helping motive. Giving thanks is the meat and fiber of prayer and the opening dialog for an individual to neutralize dissatisfaction. Being grateful for a condition that displeases you may seem strange, but with time this strategy will bring changes. The Light Warrior concept must be integrated into your self-concept. In short, you must let go of the old rigid negative concept of you, in order to take on a greater more forgiving concept of you. Accepting this idea and seeing with non-judgment is not always easy. Three methods of shape shifting a rigid concept engrained into your mental and emotional programming are:

One: (*Conquering*) get out of the head by forcing the body into **extreme physical exercise**. Extreme means to push the body to its limits beyond 11 to 31 minutes or more. The body will force you to pay attention to its physical priority thus letting go of present mental preoccupation. This is achieved with a physically exhausted euphoric state. (*Consult your physician when developing an exercise routine.*)

Two: (Surrendering) get out of the head by forcing the body into **extreme spiritual exercise**. Chanting, rapid breathing, prayer, yoga are just a few ways to release negative concepts that are firmly embedded in your thoughts. Push yourself to its limits beyond 11 to 31 minutes or more.

Three: *(Neutralizing)* replace negative mental and emotional judgements with **extremely positive mental and emotional suggestions**. This is a difficult exercise especially when dealing with strong inner judgmental criticism or people that turn, twist and reshape the truth. If there is a source of negative judgment, it must be recognized and neutralized.

The Dimension of Thought can transform your world by altering the negative into the positive, causing a massive devastating reconstruction (moments of clarity). This demands an eye open awakening to the fear you live in as well as an assault on that fear (Dragon Slaying). It is in the Dimension of Thought that Dragons are able to manifest as fears. Acknowledging fear as something real indicates that your thinking is tainted. **"To change your world you must first change your mind."** This sounds simple, right? It can be, but normally people will not change their mind until the universe can no longer accept the world that they have created. If the Dimension of Thought is overrun by ignorance, then a glimmer of light will appear as a frightening shock wave. Devastation may occur simultaneously with transformation and reconstruction. This is the Tower Card in a Tarot deck. The Light Warrior remains steadfast to what is known to be true in the midst of illusion. Continually reconfirming the simple Truth helps to maintain a clear picture of what is real so it never leaves your sight, even in the center of chaos. This is why it is important to know what is true about you. We have all heard the defense tactic, *"That's* not my fault because *this* is your fault."* This is reaction formation, and is a classic strategy for manipulating the truth. It is used to displace the blame for actions associated with weakness. So few accept responsibility for their actions because others will perceive them as weak. Too often, people will not even allow themselves to see their weakness. Accept your limitations. Overcoming weakness is a part of life's journey. How can people develop strength if they cannot recognize weakness? Recognizing and confronting your weaknesses is the walk toward enlightenment. Choose gratitude to re-balance the negative and begin a process of improvement. Blaming others for your weak behavior is an action born out of weakness itself. Your destiny depends on you cleansing your life of the sludge brought on by weak behavior. Life is a learning process and even weakness can give us a real purpose. It allows us to see our lesser concepts so we can integrate strength.

Name three characteristics in your personality that you recognize to be weak. In most cases this will be fear, seduction or addiction. In choosing, make sure that each one of these weaknesses has emerged in your life many times. Remember to remain honest without placing harsh judgment on yourself.

Define the Weakness

1.

2.

3.

These character weaknesses may have caused harm to you and to those who care about you. This exercise is to dispel the shadow by bringing it forward into the light. It doesn't need to be seen by others. Your opinion of yourself is all that is important. Look at these weaknesses and face them as yours. This can be a difficult exercise because it is a natural tendency to shut down our hearts to numb the pain of our inner critic.

Shutting down the heart, however, is a weakness also. The Third Millennium Warrior is a warrior of the heart. Do not be afraid to feel. **Keeping the heart open is a strength that requires discipline and practice.** *An open heart evolves and enhances the emotional strength of the Warrior Spirit. You must first take honest responsibility for your weaknesses in order to correct the pattern. Filter your thoughts through the heart. Find compassion for yourself within the Dimension of Thought. Without harsh self-judgment you may find that all weak behavior begins with a thought. Equally so, all strong behavior begins with a thought. The result is the alchemy of changing the negative into the positive. Let go of your concept of you and look at the illusions to which you have been clinging. Shape shifting begins with letting go of a concept. Shape shifting concludes with claiming a different concept.* Changing your mind will shift reality as you see it. Your frame of mind projects onto the realities around you. Become the teacher by being a good listener. Become the healer by healing yourself. Having healed yourself the knowledge to heal others need only be accessed from your thoughts. Within this dimension of thinking is knowledge of unlimited potential. If you can expand to think beyond programmed limitations and judgments, forgiveness is only a thought away.

LESSON TWENTY

Ego Versus Nature

Man's attempt to control the world has inevitably come down to a game of people against nature. It has been Mankind's assumption that, **"To the victor come the spoils."** Let's begin understanding this assumption by defining all the players in this game. First, there is you. Then, there is everything else. All of nature stands on one side while you stand there negotiating a deal to get what you want. After all, you want what you want and that is a good enough reason to have it, or so it would seem. The next phase of the game is justifying what you want and, of course, allowing yourself the opportunities to have it. Prosperity is a wonderful thing. We should all prosper as long as it coincides with the properties of nature. Most people will agree, however, if your Truth is contrary to your desires then this is where the danger begins. Your Truth will directly pertain to your needs, but your wants and your needs can sometimes be two different things. Who you are defines your individual journey. The journey is a one-of-a-kind creation manufactured for you. It is a tailored capsule designed and built for a single voyage. Your identity has a mission; though unique in appearance it takes you on a lifetime voyage to seek out relationships by determining common ground. Ultimately, a successful mission requires that you find your way through the darkness and into the light where we all have common ground. Unity and stability are in the light and shaky are those that cannot choose which path to take. Fear lurks in the dark like a predator waiting for you to fall back from the pack. Indecision manifests from fear and is not a part of the Kingdom of Clarity. Sometimes we even fear the power of free will. Being afraid is not a sin, but choosing to give into fear will determine your brand of sin. Seductions are not sins.

History has mislabeled sins for centuries. A sin is an error. Sin is not the temptation but the action of being weak that misleads us and causes mistakes. The Ego is credited as the reason why we sin, but this is also a mistake that has been mislabeled. The Ego has been labeled the opposite of God, yet it is God who has given us this gift of an Ego. The Ego and free will are gifts received in the same package. The concept of the "I" is the concept of the Ego. The Ego is the (i) in the center of the un-i-verse. The "I" in you is empowering and develops a sense of confidence through affirmation, for example, "I am . . . ," or "I can . . . ," or "I will . . .". The Ego is our support system that should not be feared or destroyed, simply developed correctly. The affirmation of "I am" can determine your stand, your identity and your choices. The Ego is you in the process of a decision. It's you and your individual choices. However, it's your choices that determine your sins. If you choose, "I am better than you," (vanity and pride) then you are being seduced and your Ego can reinforce the seduction while taking you on a course of self-delusion and sabotage. If you choose the opposite, "I care," (love and compassion) then you've chosen light to personify the Ego and your self-image will support this affirmation as well. If the Ego is destroyed your spirit will be broken. The Ego and your spirit must serve a higher purpose together. There is undoubtedly a dark side to the Ego, as in all God-gifts. The Ego's shadow side is caused when you choose to block your light by placing a false Prideful image of yourself in front of Truth. The shadow side can be overcome with a re-birthing process poorly labeled as "Ego Death." Ego re-birthing is a humbling process that gives power to the positive side of the Ego and develops a weapon against seduction. All that really occurs with "Ego Death" is to recall and apply the incredible power of a strategy called "Surrender." With positive affirmations such as, "I am not afraid," or, "I am strong," we correct and guide our journey to our higher self. In this way we can find confidence in ourselves and step into our power. The challenge is what we allow our Ego to support. Choosing to disrespect the greater laws of nature will surely manifest a lesson for your maturity. Humility can sometimes teach with devastating authority. Salvation is at your fingertips if your Ego is patterned after honesty, compassion and respect. It is our virtue not our control that allows human beings to live harmoniously with nature. We must no longer be a cancer to this planet. The earth is a tolerant warrior. If you wish union with her, then be more like her. The self-image of a compassionate and tolerant warrior offers harmonious results and deep impact on you and the future of our world.

LESSON TWENTY-ONE

The True Earth

Native Americans refer to the connection with the earth as "Turtle Medicine." This is a medicine of body and spirit. The beauty of the feminine spirit exists in the loving and nurturing soul of the True Earth. The very secrets of femininity are in the Earth around us and have always been there. She carries the grace of our mother, our mate, and our self. One cannot exist in balance without the feminine spirit. Balance and harmony create grace. Neither man nor woman can find grace without balance. Respect is crucial.

"If one does not respect the Earth then one cannot possibly respect themselves." *Tao Te Ching*

Many of the ancient beliefs in the mother spirit are lost and forgotten. The indigenous tribes insist on maintaining the ancient traditions of the earth mother and for that we should be grateful. Without strong examples, the value of the earth mother continues to dwindle away as luxury and comfort replace love and compassion. The Culture of the Forgotten Truth would have you believe that femininity and the earth are two different things. This arrogance is perpetuated by greed and disrespect. Today much of the True Earth lies in ruin because selfish domination continues to corrupt the hearts of shallow people. A Defender of Light must always respect the Earth. The earth's spirit and wisdom grounds us to keep us secure. A healthy earth is essential in the fight for survival and to remain free. **She is the gracious host to our experience.** We must abide by her rules and read her wisdom. If you cannot read nature's doctrine, her weather, terrain and her chain of command then you live in a delusion of false security. The True Earth provides everything necessary for victory, but if we and our leaders are not in harmony with the land then all will lay to waste and ruin. People and the earth are one; we must overcome our behaviors of separation. Union is the future and division only slows the process of evolution. Find a place in your heart today and aid the Great Mother by honoring what she offers us. If the earth is lost then hell will win "The Game" and the middle world of life is over.

The True Earth is the body that is a vessel for a great spirit. We too are a body that is a vessel for a great spirit. Many of the experiences of life are delivered through the physical portion of our journey. We indulge in the physical because it feeds our practical nature. The practical, however, is blind to our spiritual connection to this great mother of us all. Much of who we are is a living example of the earth. So much of our spirit is denied when we abuse ourselves. Our body and the earth body share a symbiotic relationship that is undeniable. Yet, in our adolescent behavior we have participated in an almost viral infestation to the earth. There are those whose life intentions represent an antibody to the virus of pollution and disease. There are others that choose the darkness of ignorance, thus poison the earth and make her sick. Some people choose to corrupt and some choose to clean. The earth as well as our body is an organism that also internally wages a war to clear and clean itself constantly from impurities. We are healing twenty-four hours a day just like the earth. The only thing that blocks both our healing and the earth's healing from reaching perfection is us. The stress, the poisons, the seductions, the unhealthy environments we accept, the unhealthy choices we make cause us to be sick. Choices created by our thoughts can distort our health. The earth and our physical self must be united as one and the same. A Defender of Light chooses a life intention that creates a healthy example for us all. Those who poison motivate the darkness of ignorance. Rise above shallow thinking to realize if we clean the earth's water of poisons, the clean water purifies us also. The clean air of the earth gives us life and energy. The clean soil gives us clean food and nourishment. Our clean intentions give the earth the potential to grow and heal to a healthy perfection. If your mental programming is seducing you into an unhealthy behavior, then exercise the beauty and potential of your body. Get out of your head and into your body. By exercising we disconnect from the mind's attachment to self-indulgence. If certain you are on the wrong path, correct the pattern through training and working out. As with the turtle, your body will protect you if you respect it. Training will offer you grace if you have the grace to work for the True Body.

LESSON TWENTY-TWO

The Quest for Virtue

"VIRTUTIS FORTUNA COMES"

The determination of every worthwhile choice should be monitored by its level of compassion and respect. Compassion and respect are two characteristics commonly referred to as virtuous. Virtue is a term that represents a mystical life force with great power and forgotten intrigue. Virtues have a spirit and vibration that should be acknowledged and honored as a reality. However, this life force requires conscious discipline to maintain its vibration. These spirits are unique in their images and exist by their own rules. They are a living force that transmits the power of Light. There are countless illustrations of gallant young warriors being lured to or from their destinies by a test of purity. These illustrations are designed to teach the reader about staying true to what is good and noble in the heart. Virtue is a resource given to help guide you to stay on your path. For centuries, it was thought to be possessed by only the elite or noble. Virtue was a word that was determined by a bloodline, wealth, nobility, and of course, abstained sexuality. However, this was another cultural misinterpretation designed with selfish intent to exclude certain magic from the less privileged. The truth is that **virtue is a grand and noble gift, but it's not offered only to the elite. It is instead, simply a higher discipline to one's greater self, designed to combat that which is common in all human beings.** That which is common is seduction. Our virtues and our seductions define us as individuals because they direct our choices. The Culture of the Forgotten Truth would convince you that virtue is lost, that there are no more honorable, honest, courageous people left. Your cultural programming would have you believe that people can not be trusted, that men and women cannot sustain friendships because of an underlying tendency for deceit, greed or lust. It is not relevant if a person feels lust or envy for a friend. It is his or her discipline not to act upon weakness that defines one's code of honor. A warrior's effort to do what is right to overcome weakness is the power of clarity. **Men and women were created as allies** and any cultural misdirection from this is simply delaying progress. The virtue of a woman is a magnificent power. History is rich with stories about men who have either killed or died to possess such a power. However, this kind of control is a childish concept. A woman defines her dignity and honor, and so does a man. Dignity and honor are not exclusive to one gender. Integrity develops self-respect and creates a powerful self-image. A strong and disciplined self-image combined with a kind heart is far too powerful for Darkness to allow. As a result, your cultural propaganda would have you believe that virtue is only a sexual term, cheating you out of the Light and magic that could be yours. The concept relative to sex is not simply abstinence, but is better defined as the discipline not to be weak when sexual impropriety is in question. Sexual impropriety is determined by core laws established as your Truth (refer to *Lesson three*). We all need discipline to live our highest Light and our purest self-image. Our virtues can counter balance our seductions such as anger, manipulations, deceptions, shame, obsession, fear, indulgence, revenge and laziness. These Nine Dragons constitute the challenges to one's character. Virtues are like playful young-hearted spirits that bring gifts and merge their power with you, but will only reside in an environment where a well-disciplined individual keeps them safe. Integrity empowers the Light Warrior.

Medieval knights were measured by their acts of purity. Percival and Lancelot were described as being so virtuous that they had the strength of ten men and could not be bested. Lancelot, however, lost his honor through an act of betrayal, and Percival became the knight pure enough to succeed at the great challenge of retrieving the Holy Grail. The Grail Knights all tried, but they were not as pure or as disciplined as Percival. This legend offers a secret magic necessary for real success. You need only open your heart to it. Discipline will help you to find your Truth and love will make it real. There is much to be learned from the stories about warriors that came before us. Draw strength from their example as the children of the future will draw strength from your story. Learn to call upon honor, respect, honesty, courage compassion and so on and apply your dedication to them. *"With virtue fortune comes"*: may this motto guide your journey because *empowered by Virtue is how you will slay your greatest Dragons.*

LESSON TWENTY-THREE

Third Millennium Chivalry

Its has been said, "Chivalry is dead." This is a false claim constructed to diminish hope and misdirect the champions of the heart. Chivalry, much like the Japanese Bushido, is a Warrior's Code and a universal truth. Darkness cannot endure a Warrior's Code based on goodness and honor. "Might for Right" is an ancient ideal which has always caused dangerous repercussions for Darkness. The core element of beauty found in Chivalry is very much alive today. It is only the gender distinction that has transformed its image. Chivalry in its purest concept represents **action for courage, honor, and good.** The service to a higher good has always been a noble profession. These beliefs are truly alive and breathing in the Third Millennium Warrior but with some modifications. Gender separation does not serve the highest power of unity. The Third Millennium woman has merited her rightful place within the warrior class. She has endured, struggled, and fought for her freedom. No greater examples can define a Defender of Light. Gender separation is why First Millennium Chivalry appears different from Third Millennium Chivalry. The Culture of the Forgotten Truth is determined to convince women that chivalry is dead when in fact it has evolved to include women as participants. The female warrior no longer is confined to be a spectator of men but is in fact a participant of the warrior's birthright. Gender separation will only slow progress and maintain the darkest hold on illusion. "Together we stand and divided we fall." There is no pure masculine man or pure feminine woman in this age. However, many will argue against this point. Fighting has never been simply a male birthright. Deep reflection on this idea is necessary for the conqueror that is both blessed and cursed with a warrior's mind. The true warrior is a warrior of self (Dragon Slayer) and the evolved warrior is a warrior of the heart (Light Warrior). The Light Warrior has fine-tuned the sensitive instincts. By developing the sensitive gifts the Light Warrior learns to move through social, religious and gender boundaries. These gifts have great powers and are available to do great things. If nothing else, sensitivity is a powerful tool in reading your enemy and is priceless in communicating with your mate. From a clearer vantage point conscious progress is possible.

In the Arthurian Age it was believed, if a king would reign in harmony with the land then all of the people would prosper. However, if the ruler did not respect or was not sensitive to the land, all would lay in waste and ruin. The abiding truth here is that if the masculine (king) is in harmony with the feminine (the earth), then the world can prosper. However, if the masculine does not respect the feminine, then the world will lay in waste. Clearly it would benefit us to adopt a philosophy of respect, especially with our planet. Men have played one archetype in the past and women played another, but this age requires gender balance. Balance requires an equalized philosophy of masculine (attaining) and feminine (letting go). Therefore, this lesson is not isolated only to men. There are women too that have lost respect for their feminine spirit and earth mother. Reflect on all the gifts you have from the True Earth. Would your life have any value at all without the earth mother and her spirit? We all require the nurturing guidance of the Earth. Listen to her and ground yourself in her example of harmony. Actions for courage, honor, and good are the qualities required for Third Millennium Chivalry. Be warned: no Chivalry exists for the warrior who serves the Religion of Darkness. Illusion is their magic. Only action for the highest good **"Might for Light"** will generate the compassionate strength that is the insignia of the Light Warrior. If you believe that you exist only on the side of a man or only on the side of a woman, then you will only serve to separate our greatest potential. Men and women were created as allies, and allies we must be in order to unite an Army of Light. The clarity of **Truth, Courage** and **Compassion** are the virtues found in the **Light Warrior**. Clarity is the way to union and peace. We must inspire the courage of the warrior to break old out-dated judgments and step forward as teachers. We must have the compassion to be able to accept other love based religions and philosophies despite their differences. Men once fought for the honor of a woman, but evolved Chivalry dictates that we fight for the honor of the feminine spirit and mother earth. Chivalry is alive in the heart of the Third Millennium Warrior.

LESSON TWENTY-FOUR

Might for Light

It has been said, in life "Only the strong survive." It would seem that strength and survival goes hand and hand, however cultural protocols create many different concepts of what basic survival means. To maintain our survival we must understand, what is real strength? Real strength in this age has taken many forms. It could be integrity, talent, stability, wealth or simply the stamina of physical ability. Old, outdated concepts of the unbending conqueror have lost their appeal for many as we make new demands on our heroic characters. Everyone has an idea of strength and weakness. Even our imperfection can be interpreted as a positive human strength. It takes an extended trial and error process to determine the contributions and retributions of how strong we honestly are. We can only hope that our strengths and weaknesses won't be too exaggerated by ourselves or by others. In the end, it's the relationships we have formed that will best reflect the virtue of our strength and power. It is important to examine how you affect all your relations, not just the successful ones but also all of them. You have a relationship with all living things, including the bond with your God and yourself. Make time for introspection and merit all of these relationships. Are there ways to improve existing relationships or is it best to surrender a failed one in the hopes that you can find forgiveness and improve the relationship with yourself? Getting correct with one's self is always a priority and the key element to every bond we make. People respond to the images we project and the images we reflect. Therefore is it possible to attract love before you remember how to love yourself? In life your visions are possible because life is a reflection of your perception. Sometimes having someone love us will remind us, that we are indeed love worthy.

Is it possible to truly find God before you can find yourself? If
God is Love and life is a reflection of your perception then
God, love and your perception have come full circle. This is a
valid point and the reason it's so crucial that you understand
who you are and what your individual Truth is. An individual's
Truth comes from one individual's perspective. It is the intention
of the Code of the Third Millennium Warrior to empower you
to stand up for who you are. The Code of the Third Millennium
Warrior has no political agenda. It only reminds you to speak
and to follow your heart. Within the Army of Light there is a
circle of equality. It consists of Light Warriors and a new age.
This was the concept of Merlin's Arthurian Round Table, where
no one sits at the head. The Round Table is intended to be
shared equally by all warriors so that no one would be judged
for speaking their heart. The Knights of the Round Table were
together as a whole and all fought for what was right. "Might
for Right" was the faithful call to arms of this ancient legend.
"Here within lives the beginning of what has always been,"
the difference is only a new age and a new age call to arms.
"Might for Light" is the call of the Third Millennium Warrior.
Might for light is, effort toward enlightenment. It is true that
the strong do survive, and your greatest strength comes from a
love of life, God and family. Love will always have the power
to conquer the worst. If you cannot love the life you have now,
then try to love the fight. **It's the fight that determines our
self-respect.** Some people are convinced that the fight is not
enjoyable; however, looking back, we all enjoyed the challenges
we've won. This is a paradox. The Culture of the Forgotten
Truth teaches you that fighting is bad, yet you know that
overcoming challenges can improve your quality of life. It is
important that we all fight. How else could we face our greatest
Dragon and overcome the fears that handicap our lives? Do
not allow cultural protocol to dictate your power. **You are as
strong as the quality of your passion.** "Might for Light" is a
fight for peace, love, and unity through nonviolence. Ask
yourself, can a person who chooses a nonviolent protest, an

individual who endures rocks and bottles and even martyrs his life for the good of others, be anything less than a great warrior? Love is strength and can help you heal the greatest wounds. Love is a gift and should not be taken for granted or betrayed. Love is Light. It's your disciplined intentions that dictate the strength of your virtue. When the cause is just, even the battle can be pleasurable. However, **if you draw your strength from anger or fear then you fight from the shadow of the Warrior.** It's a warrior's heart that beats the hardest, and if your heart is pure, then you have risen as a great example of strength for us all.

LESSON TWENTY-FIVE

Anger Displacement Syndrome

Fire Breathing Dragon

Anger is an illusive Dragon with a talent for intense transmutation. It can be manipulated into both a strategy of attack or a strategy of defense. Anger or rage is an effective method to displace blame through a smoke screen of illusion. Information given through a smoke screen makes it difficult to focus clearly on the truth, for example, **"You can't be angry at me because I am angry at you! or, I am not to blame because it is your fault!"** This is an example of the angry victim. It is an easy defense to wage because deception through aggression can achieve a powerful tactical advantage. Many are so versatile with this defense that an opponent may not even engage simply because of the perceived aggression. Rage is power and a force to be reckoned with. It can be used as a control tactic to offset blame or insecurity. Even the manipulators themselves can deceive their own point of view with a dramatic aggressive display. Many people repetitively use anger and aggression as a tool to deny their blame and responsibility. Some even displace emotional pain by using it as a technique to deceive themselves. Guilt and shame are often conveyed through an Anger Displacement Syndrome. Persecution is a form of displaced anger as is prejudice born of judgment. When internalized it creates powerful negative repercussions that can manifest into physical ailments. Cancer, disease or chronic muscular pain are just a few ailments that can manifest when it is internalized. If trapped inside it can wreak havoc. It is important not to worship it as strength. Although aggression is powerful, it is mostly a darker power. Considering it strength is a deception perpetuated by pride. Anger is a weakness unless it's channeled into productivity or compassion. Anger is only of the Light when it is filtered through the heart to seek out healing, justice or peace. This channeling is an example of pure alchemy. Anger is multifaceted and not always evil. Attaching your Truth to anger can point you or someone else in the correct direction. It is only displaced anger that wears the cloak of corruption. It can be used to a positive resolve and is capable of elevating one to a high spiritual experience. However, this is a rarity because it requires humility to use anger positively. Sometimes it can help make us choose a better life for ourselves. In many cases moving from an unhappy place gives it a purpose. It can be shifted to passion. We must begin somewhere on our spiritual journey and anger can confirm the need to begin. It too is a life force and must be freed for you to live a healthy existence. **Trapped tension is the slow corrosion of happiness.** An angry state is a sign that dissatisfaction is a part of your world. If dissatisfied, applied changes and reinforced gratitude are the only resolutions to fulfillment. In most cases, anger will find the deceptive path and be used to deny love behind an act of aggression. It can take many shapes. It can easily be reshaped to fit a just cause, however, one must remember that justice, like beauty, "is in the eye of the beholder." We must look deep to find the real reasons we feel angry.

If you are dealing with unhappy people your life is affected. The question is, what is an effective strategy to combat displaced anger in an argument? This is a battle passionately fought to create a delusion. The answer is much simpler than the act. **Anger Displacement Syndrome, or the *act* of anger to displace the truth,** has only one correct defense: to maintain the Truth without fear. Maintain Truth to expose the Dragon. The Truth will stand long after the smoke screen is lifted. Hold fast to what you know to be clear and trust in that. Faith is an important ally on the warrior's path. If you feel yourself slipping into debates with needless aggression, then remind yourself continuously of what you know to be true. Generate a force field of Light around you and recognize only the honest words will penetrate. These types of confrontations are the most frustrating for honest people, but you must stay strong. You are battling with the Fire Breathing Dragon of Anger, and this one has a burn as well as a bite. Sometimes the bite can become deadly, so be aware that it is only a short metamorphosis from rage to violence. No one but you can determine the danger. Trust in your heart and follow it. Abuse is born of anger and is definitely an evil designed to destroy your path. If you, on the other hand, are the one who displaces angry aggression to manipulate others, then understand clearly that there is much work to be done. Begin with honesty and the Art of Listening. The rest will follow.

Anger is the shadow side of the warrior. The fire breathing Dragon of Anger is an ancient and elusive creature. It slithers among the corridors of the dream world, existing in shadows and lurking in silent provocation. From the beginning of time it has been among us. Its existence is old and transmutes from parent to child, never allowing total exposure of its demon heart. People carry anger inside them everywhere they go, not realizing the force of Darkness that can be unleashed. It attaches itself to the desires of fantasy. This tactic can deceive even the most introspective. Rage has little purpose in the Kingdom of Light, yet we delude ourselves on what good things we can do if we're **provoked** into anger. This is the powerful delusion of the Anger Dragon and a distortion of divinity. Anger can, however, be clean as well as filthy. It takes true clarity to distinguish between these two expressions. It is indeed possible to only appear angry motivated by a good-hearted passionate intention. The English language has no word to separate clean anger from harmful anger. This is a testament of the Dragon's elusive power; for example, it sometimes feels good to be angry. It is easy to draw upon anger, however, it is possible to move into conflict and never unleash the Dragon. Fighting without anger is the challenge of an evolved warrior. Yes, it is possible to fight without anger, but you must search your soul for this ability. Being strong depends on the ability to stand up for yourself with self-respect; however, this self-empowerment does not depend on anger. The right, not the righteous, distinguish this fine line of clarity. Whether the ramifications are productive or nonproductive are the clues to be determined. Are the intentions selfless or selfish? Darkness eats at you and can stalk you in your dream state. If you have ever risen from a night's sleep with your jaws clenched, then you have been visited by anger's intent. This dark energy feeds on your soul and hinders your process as a Defender of Light. Dark energy brings internal angst, discontent and pain. Since there is no English word to describe clean anger, it is defined here as the passion of Light. Acting out with aggressive intent for a higher cause, for example, healing yourself, is nothing more than exercising your warrior spirit and falls within the Light Warrior's passion. However, misinterpretation of a warrior's destructive or constructive nature is a very delicate matter. **Be warned! The pools of blood run deep in our history from the ignorant that misinterpret the message of Light.** Darkness can easily seduce the "holier than thou." This is how the Dragon survives. To disguise itself as clean when it is unclean is the message of a false prophet. This is the core root of human deception. It takes the careful perception of a clear individual to determine the difference. A sheep will blindly follow those who use this deceptive tactic, but the Lion chooses a different path. A Lion will attack with forceful intent, but without malice. A Lion is simply being a creature of nature ready to protect, defend and survive. The Code of the Third Millennium Warrior requisitions you to be the Lion. It is good and healthy to exercise the warrior spirit as long as you do it with your anger in check. Respect is the key. Respect yourself, others and all living things. Staying respectful and protected by light can fend off an illusive attack from a negatively driven force. Respect can neutralize. Neutralization is the highest level of war practiced by the Ambassadors of Light.

As it is possible that sometimes a twist of fate can place you on the wrong side, a Defender of Light must stand up for what is clearly real. This is the power, courage and individuality of the Light Warrior Spirit. This is, **"Might for Light."** It is not an easy task to step outside of someone's destructive angry path. There is never anything easy about anger at all. It can feed on you internally and can be manifested externally in the blink of an eye. Staying strong when everyone else is losing his or her humanity to rage or fear will be the challenge and your moment of Truth. Changing times will rock the face of humanity and you will be responsible as a Light Warrior to represent your core convictions. Will you step forward as a beacon of Light and maintain integrity when chaos becomes normality? Will you choose the Light and be what you are destined to be? Could you pull back from anger to determine if you represent a higher image of justice? Define now which side you will serve. In battle and surrounded by chaos you just may not have the same luxury of time.

LESSON TWENTY-SIX

Reawakening the Light Warrior

The Sleeping Lion

The warrior spirit is empowerment. It is the ability to achieve and make things happen. It gives us success, victory, and prosperity. It is the energy and the potential born from pure effort. Effort is the primary ingredient necessary for success. We are the only creatures on this planet driven to succeed. We are not the only animals bred to fight but we are the ones that can develop our evolution. To "Fight" is to apply your efforts with the intent to succeed and that is why we are gifted with a warrior spirit. To merge this warrior spirit with spirituality is the combination of effort and grace. Anger, control, and fear are the shadow of the warrior not the Light. *The Light Warrior is a warrior of the heart.* The Light Warrior is a rational thinking warrior dedicated to serve humanity. A mature warrior is balanced enough to know if a challenge cannot be conquered; victory can sometimes be attained through a strategic surrender. Acceptance and letting go can sometimes determine our maturity. *The Dragon Slayer is a warrior of the self*, which is a being dedicated to overcoming the internal challenges. Being a warrior of the self (Dragon Slayer) means to face and fight our own fears, seductions, and addictions. Without the warrior spirit you have no defenses to face your fears, overcome your seductions and no discipline during weakness or addiction. The Third Millennium Warrior is the Light Warrior awakened. It is warriors of the self that are dedicated to the heart. Therefore they may never need to cause other's bloodshed or endanger themselves to achieve victory. The Light Warrior is the fourth level of the master's path. The fourth level is reached when someone takes the sum of all the work they have done on them self and chooses to help others. The fourth level of mastery is for those who made an agreement to walk in this life as a humanitarian. There are many of you who are unaware of your agreements but somehow know you have a purpose to fulfill. The new warriors have an understanding of themselves and can recognize correct action over an unbridled pride. They can go beyond childlike tantrums and clearly read a situation as it truly is. To achieve this, one must understand and develop a code of honor and be clear that fighting for victory is a way of life and fighting for a greater life is victory. If you have these qualities, you possess a strength, a cunning and a calm that cannot be calculated. You can conquer to victory, surrender to victory or neutralize to victory. What's important is the understanding of what victory is. "The end justifies the means." To live a powerful life we all must fight to get the job done. This is an ability that we have all experienced; therefore it is a talent that we all share. Some have refined it, and some have unfortunately forgotten this talent. The Culture of the Forgotten Truth would persuade you not to remember your warrior path, but warriors we all are. Most people barely remember that they even know how to fight. Sadly, this Truth is case in point for the masses that choose to be victimized sheep when God has chosen them to be lions. The Code of the Third Millennium Warrior challenges you to awaken the sleeping lion, be noble, strong and when threatened, fierce. Accept your birthright and reawaken the warrior in you. Unfortunately, there are barricades of cultural protocol that blocks our abilities to remember how. Accessing it may require a diligent effort to peel away the layers of resistance brought on by fear, blame and victimization. By diminishing all the layers of fear, you may even come to realize a fleeting distant whisper of greatness exists. Luckily, even the Culture of the Forgotten Truth cannot silence a call of greatness. This is the call of the Master within, calling you to fulfill your agreements. Ignore it and it slips back into the forgotten abyss. Move with it and you can chip through the blockage to find your lost memory. If it helps you, place yourself in the company of action people. Use your gift of strategy to position and move you forward. If your warrior memory is too faint, then plan smaller steps to greatness. It may seem that you need to overcome your problems before your destiny's journey can begin. These problems are your destiny. Accept it because these are battles necessary to arm you with strength, maturity and wisdom. This is preparation. **Your victory could happen tomorrow, depending upon the battle you fight today.** The journey may seem unreachable from where you stand, so move to a better vantage point. Know that clarity awaits you elsewhere if discord stands with you now. Higher ground has always been the preferred choice of the seasoned General.

LESSON TWENTY-SEVEN

Fear of Greatness

The Sluggish Dragon

There are those among you that have chosen the path of a Victim. The victim energy drama runs rampant along the shores of misery. It is the easiest path of all because it requires very little effort to create. Effort, however, is the mark of a warrior, and it therefore stands to reason that laziness is a mark of cowardice. If choosing never to face your fears is your choice, you bear the cowards' insignia (The mark of a Victim). **The excuses run deep for those who carry the Dragon's Mark.** Life is hard and no one disputes this; however, if you attach a lie to this Truth, you exist only in the shallow Truth of the victim's path. The deep Truth is that hardship is always a test. Do not fear the great game of life. Life is a wise and fruitful teacher with a clear message to deliver. You cannot expect to succeed if you are too afraid to play in life's game. Life's experience is not always about winning the grand prize. It is winning knowledge gained from experience that is priceless. Do not believe that failure is the only knowledge gained from failure. Success can be learned from failure. If you support failure without seeking a higher understanding; then you are indulging in misleading cultural protocol. We are taught winning is an end in itself. A Defender of Light understands that life is a balance of taking and giving. It is possible to win from a loss and lose from a win. That is why a Defender of Light cannot be defeated. All real knowledge is power and gaining power is in no way a defeat. Choosing not to try because you might lose is a religion devoid of experience. Not trying is a seduction of laziness (Sloth) that betrays your capabilities. Victory will make you happy, but loss will make you stronger. **The greatest fear** of humanity is the Fear of Greatness. This fear is a massive Dragon to slay and one that can easily overshadow the dreams of the unfocused and lazy. Few will ever overcome this Dragon because of its magnitude. So few have the courage to step into their power and feel the potential of their own Light. Why is it that those most afraid of the dark remain quivering and hiding in darkness? Have you asked yourself lately, "How can I step into my power?" Have you asked yourself, "How can I challenge myself today?" Your greatest Light may be waiting on the other side of one door, yet you hesitate. Why? Is it that you are afraid of your own Greatness? Has fear created so many layers of blocked memory that you cannot even see the Greatness in your heart? This is a travesty of the human experience. The greatest sorrows of humanity are the sins against self-expression. What happened to the poetry never read or the song never heard? What happened to the man too afraid to express his heart, or the women too afraid to voice her ideas? The Warrior Spirit is an ancient gift from God and yours to embrace. So what kind of sin does the Warrior commit who is too afraid to fight? We long for answers to this universal mystery but even the Ancient Masters are perplexed at this enigma. The power of Darkness would have you forget away your Greatness, forget away your true purpose, and forget away your right to choose. It is up to you to question belief patterns that are oppressive and self-destructive. If blame and victim energy has found a home with you then consider this affirmation a strategic recourse: "I am not a victim and I will not be victimized." The only logical course of action to an action problem is to choose action itself. The challenge is to reawaken the warrior self and face your fears with the clarity and grace Light provides. The Tao of the Dragon Slayer challenges your inner dragons. Face them and see them for what they are. Is it possible laziness is the seduction that hinders your success? Could hard effort have overcome past failures? Cultural misinterpretation has clouded the Warrior's path with corruption. It offers you an illusion without effort. This

Corruption of Truth has laid the groundwork for laziness to grow. You know it, you see it, and there is even a distant voice that has told you to get up and take charge of your success as a warrior on your path. That is the voice of the Ancient Masters calling you to Greatness. Listen to it. It will guide you home. Open your heart to the possibility of achieving your imagination. Visualize the victory. Remove the blocks and collapse time between now and success. Fight with courage for your greater self and greatest truth. **To fight for the Truth (Courage) is the 4th challenge of the Light Warrior.**

LESSON TWENTY-EIGHT

The Art of Doing

The results necessary to achieve effortlessness are a culmination of persistent effort with a relaxed implementation (effort and grace). Repetition is the key to attaining effortlessness, and hard work breeds this resolve. A warrior's effort is the spark that ignites this flame. No worthwhile task is achieved without someone's applied effort. Lack of effort is sitting and waiting for God to ignite the flame when God has ordained you to be the match. When it comes to achievement, western philosophy often focuses on the **bottom line** outcome. In eastern philosophy, it is the **process or journey** that has value. The Art of Doing places a much broader picture on the bottom line, thus exemplifying the balance of both philosophies. Doing and achieving become one and the same as the two ideals intertwine in a much more tolerant strategy of accomplishment. Being patient means more forgiving, with the acceptance of responsibility lingering in the distance. Fanatical obsession is a loss of balance, because as one thing ascends something else descends. Wealth, for example, can undoubtedly buy more freedom in this society; however, donating all your free time pursuing wealth is contradictory. Balance must set a precedent. The Art of Doing is accomplishing through balance. People are motivated by either fear or pleasure. Fear-based accomplishment always pays a price. You must do what you enjoy or find a way to program yourself to enjoy what you do. The goal is healthy physical, mental, emotional and spiritual growth. Balance of the four worlds is the key that unlocks the doors to prosperity. It is important to keep in mind the value each of the four worlds have in your life. We must give ample respect to each and all. If one of the four worlds is slighted an imbalance will occur. A conscious pursuit of each and all is necessary to maintain progress and healthiness. Admittedly, work does not always make us happy; however, Good work does lead to healthiness and healthiness **can** make us happy. **The Art of Doing is to approach necessary obligation with grace, ease and commitment.** This soft-style method of fighting may seem paradoxical but it is far less threatening to the body, mind and soul. Ease into your daily tasks as if easing into an old pair of slippers. This is the conquering through surrendering and the surrendering to victory strategy. Dance is a good example of the Art of Doing. Dance is effortlessness attained through diligent practice. **See life as a dance.** Going to work each day is the essence of the Art of Doing. Being self-motivated is far more efficient if you **allow** yourself to want to do the work, as opposed to forcing yourself to do the work. It is then that your work or your career becomes a part of who you are. Instead of something separate, you can refer to work as your lifestyle, or life practice, for example, "I'm not going to work I'm just doing what I do." Doing is moving and motion is the way of the Universe. If stagnated, the Universe will force a move and in some cases abruptly. Don't wait, stop or wonder. Just move into and with the process easily. Reprogram yourself to relax and **breathe** at the initial moments of self-motivation, then ease into the correct direction. When fully immersed, you can allow yourself to build momentum. The Art of Doing is an art form designed to combat procrastination. Procrastination is a tactic of the Sloth Dragon and difficult to combat because it depletes our energy. Maintaining energy over this Dragon is the only way to defeat it. As a warrior and Defender of Light, you must hold on to your passion and give no one the ability to deplete your energy. The world is full of vampires and many will try. Victimization, blame, excuses, procrastination or just plain laziness are the images of the Sloth dragon. Energy is necessary to stay on your path and to represent your way in the Army of Light. You have the potential and the power to lead people to Light, that is, if you can find it. All that is necessary is Clarity,

Courage and Compassion. Unfortunately to attain these virtues is a challenge for all of us. The challenge will lead you to your destiny, but first you must take on the challenge. The next step could be simple if you: Relax, breathe, and then Make It Happen. The dance of life is every morning lifting your spirit gracefully to get in the game. Ease your way toward being an example of balance and honesty. Doing what is necessary may not seem pleasurable, but will lead you to pleasure. Live a good example and you will unite your community. Bringing together people is the beginning of a peaceful shift, but this is only possible if you can first relax, breathe calmly, and then, **get in the game.**

LESSON TWENTY-NINE

The Art of Listening

The demeanor of silence before and during the act of listening is what opens a portal to the Dimension of Thought. To engage the silence is to dedicate effort to your education. Listening is a martial art because it requires serious discipline, with the resolve of enlightenment. Listening is a hidden technique beneath all art forms and is essential for receiving information from teacher to student. **Focused listening is the dedication to conscious learning.** Choosing to be an expert listener is accepting a challenge that is dedicated to mastery and respect. Listening is a courtesy that equates to respect and is a neutralizing force that can diminish the evils of separation and bigotry. The power of the Word is giant, but if you do not pay attention then you have learned nothing and missed the point. "To miss is a sin." To sin through habit is poor judgment and the recreation of fools. Poor judgment is the first action of hellish demise. However, good judgment is based on education, which requires learning, which requires listening, which requires a personal silence. If you have difficulty with inner silence, then your next assignment is to be quiet. Continue reading and allow your inner silence to acknowledge your inner voice. Your inner voice has a subtle and yet familiar wisdom. It is analyzing this information and making the appropriate determinations for this experience. Engaging the inner voice connects you to your master within. We all have an inner master, but all too often we forget to listen to our own sound advice. This wisdom is our guiding light. It is our soul and wiser self. If all you hear is inner criticism, try to delve deeper. The inner master has a kind, loving voice.

A proficient listener will form stronger relationship bonds. Thus all relations prosper. Over time, good listeners develop a rational thinking process based on the assessment of information earned through their own induced silence. Listening is an Ego check designed to reestablish the balance lost through self-absorption. It is a multifaceted talent incorporated into all relationships. Proficiency with this skill should be developed. As it is developed so does the ability to understand others through your listening to your own inner self. There are many levels to inner hearing; for example, listening to your body can prevent physical problems. Listening to your gut instincts can prevent horrible disaster. Listening to your heart allows love to guide your path. Your inner voice is designed for introspection, intuitive perceptions and creativity, as well as developing strategy and resolving mental or emotional issues. Listening to the people in front of you allows the assessment of knowledge to materialize. **On every level of relationship, the Art of Listening is a valuable discipline that perpetuates knowledge,** and as you know, "Knowledge is power." Therefore, it will also develop power. **Listening and remembering** go hand in hand for the quest of Truth. This is an important key to hear and remember on the path to self-empowerment.

Having said all that, we can now move beyond the physical and mental voice. We can even move beyond our personal relations for a true test of perception. Listening to the divine, your highest source of creation is, by definition, creative inspiration. "Creativity is the highest form of intelligence." Divine revelation links us to God. Ignore it and you have turned a deaf ear to heaven, earth and beyond. Divine inspiration is the current of energy that empowers the human spirit. We must develop as receivers to hear the transmitter. In time the connection becomes one and the two are not separate. Try to recall the memory of when you were touched by a creative force. Open your heart to that creative passion. Can you recall the experience of imagination flowing like power? Opening and listening to the heart through conscious effort is the key that unlocks the gateway between heaven and earth. This kind of practice helps develop the ability to hear the messages of divine revelation more clearly. Opening your creative process aids in accepting spiritual messages. Listen intently to your mental, physical, emotional and spiritual self. Ask your inner guide questions and be patient. What is being said? Attempt a deeper relationship by listening to the sound of nature and the awe of her beauty. Listen to the lessons learned from the past. Listen to the wisdom of silence. What do you hear? "In the end all Truths will be known." That is, with all due respect, if you are listening.

LESSON THIRTY

Ancestral Memory

The person-to-person connection is the strongest and most complex system of patterns within a magnificent framework we call a relationship. The complexity of the relationship is a driving force for humanity to learn and grow. The methods in which we comprehend, manipulate, and control relationships can be traced back through our bloodline and ancient memory. **Bloodline transference of memory is known as Ancestral Memory.** This is the information downloaded from your parents that was downloaded from their parents and their parents before them. This information can be positive, but in most cases people tend to focus heavily on the negative. It is easy to blame our flaws on our predecessors; however, this only serves to recognize our issues of weakness. **Blaming your life's failures on others is a weakness in itself.** Blame is taught to us by the Culture of the Forgotten Truth. Every time we blame others we send the message that we are not responsible for the "goings on" in our life. A warrior learns discipline over one's destiny and develops strength from taking responsibility of one's life. All weakness within your character should be approached like a hunter tracks down its prey. Seek it out, face it, and then put it to rest. Parent blaming, a widely practiced pastime, is as reckless as giving away your gift of free will. Gender blaming as well as race, color, and religion blaming also is a widely practiced pastime. Even when the intentions seem harmless, blaming forfeits personal control and this victim energy concept will only delay your process as a warrior. It is a true warrior who can turn a loss into something powerful and beneficial. The warriors who are able to snatch victory from the experience of defeat are the true Defenders of Light. The warrior birthright is also a memory passed down. It was the ancient Masters that preserved the Martial Art teachings in order to transmit the warrior birthright through centuries of time into a culture that would deny its people their warrior spirit.

In some way all people come into this world with ancestral iniquity. The bloodline memories challenge us all to complete the mission our parents or our greater parents did not. Looking at the efforts, trials and misfortunes of those who came before can give us direction of who we are today. However, you are newer, stronger and clearer, born in a different time with the advantage of having a higher vibration to call upon. You can complete the circle and conclude the ancestral mission started long ago. This is your time. The trick is to challenge yourself to find the fear or seduction that tripped up those who came before you. Then empower your discipline and focus to attack seduction's plan. Conquer, surrender or neutralize this Ancestral Dragon that has attached itself to your family and to you. Try to remain impartial and non-judgmental towards your parents. They too wanted to be greater than they are, but like everyone, they were seduced out of their greatness by the power of weakness. If you become stuck, let go of the concept you exist in. Surrender is an action and therefore requires a warrior's effort also. It is your turn now to break the patterns of self-destruction that have attached themselves to your lineage. Take on this battle willingly and with an open heart. A delay could put it off onto the next generation. Call upon the greatness of your birthright to fight, which also passed down through your bloodline from your parents. Call upon the warriors of your Ancestral Memories. Imagine all the warriors of your bloodline rising up to combat the Ancestral Dragon. Imagine a magnificent battle between good and evil, concluding for all eternity that you are the greatest defender of your family's name and honor. You alone will step onto the battlefield and take on the evil that is waiting to corrupt your children. This Dragon is patient and is eager to snatch up the offspring of the next generation in the same way it locked in on you. Will you take on the challenge or will you also give in to the seduction of negativity in your family. This is a big challenge with a powerful Dragon. Are you strong enough this time to end the patterns of self-destruction that can only rob you and your children of their greatness? If you end the pattern you are not the only one healed. Your parents and all of your ancestral bloodline taste the victory. The rest of us will also benefit from your example. Within you is a memory. It may be faint, but it exists. This memory stores who you once were and defines the power and balance needed to attain what you were always meant to be.

LESSON THIRTY-ONE

Stubborn Enchantment

Earth Dragons

The Earth Dragons are rigid and illusive in nature. They feed on inflexibility and the refusal to budge. They are our fears, seductions and addictions that we won't let go of. The strategy of the Earth Dragon is one of immovable foundation and persuades us to hang on to old illusions or perfectionist ideals. It is the **fantasy** that things would be perfect *"If only you were this* or *If* only *I had that."* This illusion that "The grass is greener", causes us to lose sight of the wondrous miracles that the day has to offer. Envy is a dragon that can take many forms, all of which will lead to discontent. Envy is wanting what others have or wanting what we don't have. Envy is a seduction to desire the unattainable perfect scenario. It is a weakness to take for granted your life. Dreaming what life would be like if the past had been different pulls us off the path of achieving a richer quality of life. It is okay to want more, but it is better to live more. Thoughts create magic and thinking solely on the unchangeable past, misdirects that magic toward non-production. "Misfortune is a human condition, without misfortune we would not be human." *Tao Te Chung*

The flaws in our personality are as important as the flawlessness. Perfectionism can cause us to become stuck for fear of making a mistake. Individuality is what makes us powerful. We will never be completely perfect and yet we are perfectly complete. Seeing oneself without judgmental perfectionism is equally as important as seeing other people without judgmental perfectionism. The idea of the one soul mate can place way too much perfection on an individual's standard. We have many soul mates, guides, and teachers. They will all teach us different things. The process of life is more like a musician playing music; there are many movements to fit a moment. Unfortunately life is also like musical chairs, where you stop is where you are. **Stubborn Enchantment is our habitual attraction to the same lesson or circumstance.** As a result we deny ourselves the new experiences of the now. The inability to break old negative patterns is an easy trap to fall into and, for the most part, can harbor our worst intentions. Breaking free from this cinched grip requires persistence and clarity. Old fears, old pain, old resentment, old unhealthy ideas, etc., are what makes us old and are the aging process in action. Hanging on to out dated ideas will add years to your life by robbing you of new value. Letting go of the past is the very thing that delivers us into the present and into a newer world of experience. Many people suffer in horrible fixed lives due to this Stubborn Enchantment. This dragon's thirst is unquenchable and will completely handicap you by denying you of living in the moment. He dominates by seducing you into reliving fears, anger, shame and unhealed emotional wounds that have long sense expired. By reliving a negative emotion like resentment, or guilt, you breathe life back into the Dragon only to allow it to devour your world. This Dragon is capable of deep infestation. Only you can discover the depth and influence of these stubborn ideas. It or they may be submerged as deep as your childhood memories. They can even go back to ancestral memories and beyond. Fear is difficult to trace sometimes, as is the anger it manifests. A Dragon is a shape-shifter and fears can take on many forms. It takes clarity to recognize that your core circumstances are the same as the previous stories you keep recreating. The people involved with your daily issues are here to teach you something. What is important is that you learn to overcome the older and unnecessary patterns. How many times has your progress been paralyzed because you just couldn't move on? How many times have you looked back on wasted years as a result of stubbornness? **(Self-absorption is the dwelling of an illusion to death.)** If this sounds like you, then you may have difficulty with the Strategy of Surrender. The Culture of the Forgotten Truth does not teach the surrender strategy. People have been lulled into believing that surrendering is weak and, as a result, historians have documented thousands of years of stubborn reoccurrence. History repeats itself over and over because we continue to perpetuate patterns. Wars can go on for generations because people can't let go of hate. Letting go gives us the flexibility to reach beyond our stubbornness. Understandably, our personalities are formed by our memories and good, bad or ugly, memories make us unique. "Do not discard the baby with the bath water". Open your heart to the flexibility and the possibilities of surrender. Are you strong enough to say, "I WANT TO FORGIVE AND I WANT TO MOVE ON"? Have faith in the infinite wisdom of divine love. Leave behind the wreckage and carnage of the past. It serves only as a library of documented education. As a source of positive learning there is no greater teacher than past experience. However, using our past as a vehicle to unlock negative emotions, mistakes and seductions can be over-indulged into a punitive fixation. If your past haunts you, then the Dragon has broken through the perimeter. The shadow side of your passions will threaten you. You have a chance if you can let it go. Seek out experiences devoted to inner peace. Exercise the Art of Forgiveness with repetition. Make forgiveness a pattern of your past, present and future. Neutralize the negative seductions by replacing thoughts with positive effort. Take time to reflect on what is good in your life if necessary. This will defy the dragons of stubborn habit. If there are issues with people you are holding on to, facing the Dragon to voice your truth is the method advocated by the Code of the Third Millennium Warrior. Speaking your heart can sometimes release the negativity. Speak your truth, but not as a victim or a victimizer; claim it as a responsible human being. Getting closure on a relationship is sometimes the most difficult lesson to learn. Rebirth awaits the conclusion of a dead process. As long as you are stuck in the old concept, new ones are put on hold. Benefiting from the past, and still moving ahead is finding the balance that exemplifies the Tao of the Dragon Slayer. Find a new way to love the old relationships. Find a new way to love the old you. Old and new, we must find a balance as with conquering and surrendering; we must accept the appropriate course of action and learn to ease our way into learning and growing. Gracefully we find new ways to love and move through old stubborn beliefs. Write old ideas down and burn them in prayer or ceremony. Make new habits that defy old ones. Replace nonproductive self-indulgence with positive hard work. If you're locked in the past you will not be fully grateful in the present. In turn if you are grateful for your present life you will not become stuck in the past. The opposite of shadow is light and the opposite of stubborness is flexibility. Flexibility gives us freedom and freedom is always the primary objective.

LESSON THIRTY-TWO

Programming

Within the dimension of thought we have an inner chatter. Some refer to it as an inner critic. In some people this inner critic can reach an almost debilitating level. This critical ongoing inner propaganda can diminish self-respect through harsh judgment. We all develop at a young age a set of core laws (truth), which we define as the self. Understanding our core laws develops a right action and wrong action structure that guides us in making decisions. These laws are programmed much like a computer is programmed. The computer is created in our image and gives us an excellent visual reflection of how we mentally process. Some programs work well while others become forgotten in some memory void. The more we are aware of how the programming works the more we grow and mature.

Maturity is achieved when a person's needs shift to a person's wants. Both then become one, for example, "I most want what I most need." It is understandable that knowing your desire is fundamental to understanding how your programming works. Desire is a multifaceted method of motivation and the root of desire should be determined and analyzed. Desire is another of the powerful gifts from God and as all God-gifts has a seductive shadow side. It's a common practice to convince oneself that our desires are necessary, only to realize later that the desire did not pertain to our real path. On the other hand many will never explore their passions due to their inner critic. It is up to you to discover if your *wants* should be unearthed. In some cases, trial and error is the only way to know. Misguided errors do have their purpose referring to the necessity of learning a good lesson. If a lesson is learned, then there is indeed value. However, in the grand scheme of things, people in general spend a lifetime recreating an unhealthy mechanical pattern over and over again. **Never learning beyond your habitual behavior is the definition of ignorance.** Yet, we make the same mistakes time and time again. It usually comes down to *wants* and *needs* or *wants* versus *needs*. For example: You may *want* the chocolate cake but your body *needs* protein. Which will you choose? Yes, it again falls into the category of freewill choices. Another example is that you may *want* to stay out all night when what you *need* is to get to bed early. Which will you choose? Inadvertently, this is defined as a test of maturity. The clear and mature choice is made when *needs* take priority over *wants*. However, this doesn't have to be a struggle. Changing your way of thinking (programming) is what changes your habitual behavior, for example, "I *want* some protein rather than the cake because my body *needs* it." Another example is, "I *want* to get to bed early rather than stay out because this is what I *need*." Making healthy or unhealthy choices (light or dark) is not a strange concept to grasp. Achieving the union of healthy *wants* and healthy *needs*, however, is a little more challenging. Balance is essential because balance creates peace. In many cases this requires effort to reprogram old patterns but in most cases this will happen gradually and timely with age. Reprogramming consciously can be achieved through post-hypnotic suggestion, repeated affirmations, prayer, meditation or retrained behavior. The subconscious mind is very childlike and requires repeated guidance to attain a response. The trick is to affirm positively in a conscious state and not negatively in a conscious or semiconscious state. Effort is the primary requirement of the Code of the Third Millennium Warrior. It is designed as a method of willful and positive reprogramming. Reprogramming is done through conscious conquering and subconscious surrendering. Reprogramming yourself to the image of your liking is the goal. This is not to program everyone to be the same, but just the opposite. Program yourself to be greater as an individual. It is designed to break free of mainstream repressed propaganda. This can be done by one person or with the help of other people. All that is required is the desire to better oneself followed by the will to act. To better yourself you may want to release various habits that no longer apply to the person that you need to be. This is all accomplished with the creative inspiration of self-improvement. There are many mysteries of the subconscious mind, and understanding this process requires much dedication. Never be afraid to delve beyond the surface because, pursuing clarity you step into the power of Truth. For the most part, there is a rational reason for these old patterns to be there. It is up to you to find out the deeper meaning and then gracefully express gratitude to free it from your world. Yes, gratitude! The inner critic believes it is a protection mechanism designed to help you and keep you on track. It is programmed to confront you and guide you much like a stern parent. Even the most difficult patterns are designed as a fail-safe built in for some sort of protection. Understanding this first is how the mystery is revealed. Pursue your journey with this question. What are the core laws that are really involved with my mechanical behavior? You may come to find it has little to do with what you thought. For example, an allergy can be the product of some fear or guilt programming from an earlier time. Excess weight could be a way to punish yourself. Bad relationship choices may be a lack of self-love. As strange as this sounds, the subconscious is trying to achieve something that you thought you wanted, not needed. Some of these programs may be based on a piece of information that is beyond your experience in this lifetime. However, do not become overwhelmed by this idea. It is important to realize we all can correct negative habits. That's why you are living now. Begin now with what you know to be real. Because love is real it is the perfect beginning. You must show love for the pattern and the inner critic. You must realize both pattern and critic's misguided intentions are trying to help. This help may have served you well in the past but now the program **is outdated** and should be updated. The heart is designed as the perfect alchemist's tool. It can transform judgment into justice. It can turn your harsh inner critic into an old dear friend that will listen to reason. Love must replace the friction between you and your critic. A dialogue of compassion for this stern critical voice in your head will begin to neutralize its negative feedback. Ultimately it is just a program of negative motivation. What is necessary to balance the negative is a program of positive reinforcement. When the negative and the positive are in balance we have peace. Once this occurs a surgical removal of the pattern is then possible. Healing is sometimes based on removing layers of programs. Sometimes old patterns exist because we can't see them through the covering of layers. Love, however, can shine light on hidden mysteries. With light, compassion, and courage, healing is a stones throw away. This is all possible within the mysteries of your own mind.

LESSON THIRTY-THREE

Reprogramming

Meditation

1st

Light candles, incense and play soft instrumental music. Non-verbal music is better because the conscious and the subconscious mind can sometimes lock on to the lyrics and story relayed in a song. Find a relaxed place of comfort. Lie down on your back with your hands by your sides. Close your eyes and focus on your breath. Breathe through the diaphragm. For more energetic results speed up the breath with quick bursts from the diaphragm until you reach a euphoric state (breath of fire). The goal is to quiet the thinking mind. Void of thought (Zen) allows the rigid concepts of yourself to be released. Focusing only on the breath allows one to stay in the present moment. Extreme breathing will raise vibration and give you an opportunity to work on yourself from a higher place.

2nd

Once the breathing has taken you to a euphoric release (eleven to thirty-one min.), imagine a white light at your toes and moving up your body very slowly. As your breathing slows, inhale light and exhale tension. The light should induce a tingling relaxed sensation in its path. Allow the light to spread up your body, triggering and activating each of the seven chakras (energy centers) located in and around your spine.

1st. Sexual organ   (grounding & creative energy center, physical sexual)

2nd. Below naval, spleen (emotion center, self, ego, emotional sexual)

3rd. Solar Plexus   (power center, warrior, courage)
4th. Heart   (love, compassion, healer)
5th. Throat   (communication, truth center, messenger)
6th. Third eye   (intuitive, clarity center, peace maker)
7th. Crown   (mystic, divine, light)

3rd

When fully immersed in light and relaxed, make this statement three times: "There is something I want to change about myself and **that something is** . . . ."

4th

Ask your inner master to provide some kind of image with which you can communicate. The image should represent **that something you wish to change.** The image can be anything that helps represent the original program that was implemented long ago.

5th

Thank your inner guide for the image you requested. Create a dialog with the image by asking if it is willing to communicate with you. You must be completely open to your intuitive. Release your practical judgment. Pay attention to your initial response. Do not second guess, just flow. This exercise requires patience. If it is not working go back to your breathing exercises until you are ready. If it is working, continue on.

6th

Thank the image for communicating and ask the image to take you back to when it was created.

7th

Thank the image for responding and ask that image what is it that it wants? The answer could be a number of things such as security, power, peace, truth, knowledge, love, perfection, grace or any one of a ten thousand different things that are unique to you.

8th

Thank that image for that answer. Communicate to the image, "If you had the thing you want then what would you want next?" This is a technique designed to shed layers and delve deeper into the self. Continue to repeat this process over and over because it may take many layers to get to the core issue.

9th

When you have reached total silence, you have reached the central issue. Immerse the central or primary issue with light, thank it, give it love and then set it free.

LESSON THIRTY-FOUR

The Philosophy of Gratitude

Within the kaleidoscope of human behavior, the experience most often taken for granted is simple gratitude. The amount of joy created by this basic method of philosophy is paramount in everyone's life, yet it's easily forgotten. There are miracles abundant unleashed by opening the heart and being grateful for the wondrous gifts of life. Being ungrateful, however, is the Dark side of happiness. There is no joy in life when dissatisfaction is the product of your labors. All of life's experiences are here to guide you and this is a blessing in itself. **Happiness exists within Gratitude.** Being thankful is a part of being whole. Giving thanks is a magic that elevates a simple prayer into a perfect miracle. All miracles are perfect and we are flowing in a river of miracles that is constantly in motion. It's the ungrateful that are blind to the miracles around them. Is it that difficult to feel gratitude for the failed relationship that was all wrong from the beginning or would you rather stew in shame or anger? Is it that difficult to look beyond the faults of a friend or mate to be grateful for the gifts that they do possess? Is it so difficult to surrender the lies of the Culture of the Forgotten Truth? It is these lies that persuade people to have an insatiable appetite that will never be fulfilled. An insatiable appetite to possess will not lead you to contentment. Being grateful is truly the opening dialogue to contentment. Grateful dialogue speaks a language that is pleasing to human ears and to the ears of God. When thanks are given in meditation or prayer for something that is yet to happen, gratitude is transformed into the magic of Faith. "Faith can move mountains". Giving thanks to Spirit is as old as time, yet so many still pray in "Wants" and "Needs." Most prayers incorporate the message, "I want this," or "please God, I need that." These types of prayers send loud bellows of laughter up from the underworld because you have been deceived by Darkness. If you pray in wants or needs, all you get is a heightened since of "Want" or a heightened sense of "Need". The gifts you seek may very well manifest if your heightened senses inspire you to go out and retrieve them for yourself. This type of prayer is only desire that perpetuates desire. Try being grateful for the wonderful things that you have and that are coming, i.e., "I have what is needed and I am gratefully expecting to get even more." **Herein lies the magic of manifestation**. Giving thanks for what is to come develops the positive faith that it will come. It is not trickery or some black magic but a conscious choice to seek out and accept a more pleasurable life, a life for which you alone would be grateful. Everyone, including the Holy Spirit, takes pleasure in giving a gift if the gift is appreciated. Appreciation is the spirit of a gift received well, and we all deserve that. Life is a gift, and why shouldn't you have the gift of a happy life? The truth is that with the gift of life there are many God-gifts such as honor, warrior spirit and love. There are God-gifts that you have not claimed that are waiting for you to step forward. Have you ever received a gift and been disappointed? Think upon the image of unsatisfied children spoiled and pampered to a fault. Do you play this role in life? What if you and only you had a magic wand and were able to transform your life into something of wondrous proportion? What if you were able to enjoy life for all the incredible gifts that have been given you? What if you had a single wish granted to you by a magic genie? Would that wish not be for happiness? What if happiness was possible just by changing your point of view? The most difficult task for warriors and victims alike is to change their mind, yet this achievement may offer victory to your doorstep. Is it not worth it to surrender stubborn habits and simply toss the behavior of ingratitude and then claim a life with victory, prosperity and appreciation? What would you look like if you woke up every morning grateful and happy? This concept may only tease your imagination; however, the imagination is the key to unlocking the mysteries of the universe. What if Gratitude was the first thing taught to us when we were young? What if Gratitude could be taught in schools to our children? What if all religions, all races, colors, nationalities and gender where to incorporate the Philosophy of Gratitude into their belief structures? If this were possible would the next generation have to contend with blame? What if the mysteries of the universe would come to light simply by saying thank you, thank you, thank you? If nothing else, we can all be grateful for our imagination.

LESSON THIRTY-FIVE

The Path

According to Taoism "All of heaven and earth shine for thee who have found the true path." The question is, "How does one find the true path?" This question is valid because most people are unaware if they are on or off it. Generally people fall within three basic levels of the spiritual journey: The asleep, the awake and the evolved. Being asleep or unaware is not uncommon but can be remedied simply by the desire for knowledge. If you have a desire for knowledge, welcome to the journey. Those who fall into the awake level have recognized their Light but have only chosen to observe the spectacle. The awake can be the most obstinate at times because they, like a pre-teenager, have just enough information to create dispute and judgment. The evolved, however, are those who are awake and are willing to do the work. Doing the work and clearing the Path requires discipline and a dedication to honesty. It also requires compassion and forgiveness. There are millions of people who are awake, but fall short because of weaknesses such as hypocrisy, judgment, fear and seduction. Because the awake people are clear enough to see good and bad, they can move easily into quick judgment. The evolved people, however, see clearly and choose integrity with the effort of forgiveness. Judgment must be filtered through the heart to find real justice. Justice is a fair judgment based on the compassion of all things involved. It takes serious *effort* to pursue a higher Light and move forward on your soul's Path. If you are uncertain of what your path is, the Path is referring to **the journey of achieving your true purpose.** Your true purpose is who you are, your Truth, your Light, etc. Because your choices have a rippling affect, this heavily affects the quality of relationships that you form along the way. Everyone has a unique life but the common factor of all paths is the lessons learned from relationships. In the end we will judge ourselves and possibly be judged by the behavior of **every** relationship that we make. A Light shines from the center of one's life and there are many ways to reach it. The core issues of the center are a combination of love, truth, peace and action, which are the core issues of the human heart. Everyone offers his or her unique viewpoint. One man may become a Priest, another a husband and father, a doctor or an artist. The choices are infinite. Choosing your path is usually either a personal desire or a process of elimination. All of us are on a path, whether we know it or not, and paths cross and intertwine in a constant, never-ending cycle of events. It is no strange coincidence that when you dive deeply into an issue, people of like interest with information appear almost miraculously. Happenstance, coincidence, miracle, magic or synchronicity is all the same and all a part of your journey to engage, learn and teach. Ultimately, union will complete a collective puzzle of which you are very much a part. The Code of the Third Millennium Warrior is specifically designed to unlock ancient memory and provoke a thinking process that channels this idea of a Path. Like the Arthurian Knights seeking adventure, this concept has been unsheathed again for a new and more dramatic age. The core issues are the same. The same questions apply for the warrior who sought destiny centuries ago as to a new age of warrior seeking the next level of awakening. The choices are still, "Should I represent the highest level of good or should I indulge in lower levels of seduction? Can I stay fixed on my virtue or will I slip hopelessly into my own addictions or imprison myself with fear." Take a moment to ask, what gives you fulfillment? What are your true talents and what do you have to offer? These are always important factors in determining your truth and defining your path. Everyone has something to offer, this is a Law and it is without exception. All people happen for a reason because "all things happen for a reason." Figuring out the reasons is sometimes the most difficult part of the journey. Try to keep it simple.

Very few of us were meant to be a President or an Ambassador. Therefore, do not underestimate your talents. We all have the ability to share our gifts, and we all represent a piece of the puzzle. Self-awareness is necessary to understand one's own true value. However, if the answers are not obvious, then we will proceed to a deeper level of truth by applying a formula of clarity, courage and compassion. If you are still uncertain how to define your path or what your real purpose is, then let's break it down for observation because value and self worth must be established to find your Path.

The Path II

If you are uncertain of your true talents or how they apply to you in your present situation we can try a different approach. In this lesson we will work to explore your unique path as it unfolds the mysteries of your story.

#1. Think of a person or persons you care about and respect. Now ask yourself, what is the image you would hope or want them to have when they think of you? Try to focus on the positive and stick closely to the image you **wish** they had of you, not necessarily the one that exists.

#2. Make a list in the center column on the next page describing this image of you with at least seven characteristics for example: strength, honesty, kindness, loyalty or generosity. Maybe it is simply joy, playfulness or success and so on. This is a good starting point because now we can focus in on an **image**. Try to be clear here because pride can easily delude this exercise with a false perception. After all, introspection is a private and personal exercise not intended for harshly judgmental evaluations.

_____ A. _____ y / n_____
_____ B. _____ y / n_____

	C. _____	y / n _____
_____	D. _____	y / n _____
_____	E. _____	y / n _____
_____	F. _____	y / n _____
_____	D. _____	y / n _____

#3. Circle **y** (Yes) by each description that is accurate today, and circle **n** (No) if you're a work in progress.

	A.	honest	**(y)** / n _____
_____	B.	carefree	y / **(n)** _____

#4. To the Yes answers, in the left column write what you did to achieve this image and complete your goals.

Discipline myself

not to lie	A.	honest	**(y)** / n _____
_____	B.	carefree	y / **(n)** _____

#5. With the No answers, in the far right column write what you need to do or what you are doing to achieve the goals that illustrate the description of the center image.

Discipline myself

not to lie	A.	honest	**(y)** / n _____
			Yoga / have
			more faith /
_____	B.	carefree	y / **(n)** ***be less critical***

#6. Using this method examine how you've succeeded in being who you are and how you are working on being who you want to be. This should begin to unfold a process. Focusing heavily on the process and starting in the left column, this should give you a past (what you've done). The center column is the present (what you want) and the far right column is the future (what could or should you be doing).

If done correctly, exercising honesty, a life story emerges about your journey to your higher self. Now take a good look at it. These are your personal achievements in the eyes of a respected opinion. It is a story of personal priorities. What do you see? The answers should suggest your **Personal Path.**

_____ past _____ A. ___ present ___ y / n___ future _____

(Y) I am ___*honest*___ because . . . I *Discipline myself not to lie*
(N) I am becoming ___*carefree*___ because . . . I am doing *Yoga / having more faith / being less critical*
Below, using your list of seven write, I am . . . or I am becoming . . . and explain why?

Example:

"I am *honest* because I have disciplined myself not to lie. I am becoming more *carefree* by doing Yoga, exercising more faith and being less critical of myself and others".

1.
2.
3.
4.
5.
6.
7.

#7. Now for a different test; from your point of view write three things that you wish you had more control over or maybe even feel stress about in your present life situation.

A._____ B._____ C._____

Of these three things, which ones have nothing to do with the original list of seven? Do these three even apply to the earlier list of your highest personal priorities? If not then ask yourself "How can I feel bad about not developing power over something that is not one of my personal priorities"? Observe the illusion of unfulfilled desire due to a lack of priority. Review back to what is needed to achieve your goals in the original list of seven, here is where your heart is guiding you. Now write a method of achieving your three desires by using some of the characteristics from your original list of seven. Success is easier when we understand how our path works and then apply our priorities and talents to the equation. Try not to stray from your path.

A.
B.
C.

LESSON THIRTY-SIX

The Path Beyond

The distance between who you were, who you are and your highest self define your journey. Do not be discouraged if you do not feel perfect; we are all a work in progress. As an artist learns with the creative process, it is important to both honor and value the process itself. The Art of Doing is highly relevant. There is a past, a present and a future to your path, and it is important to know where you have been to realize where you're headed. If your highest self is an image of good, then you have established a pathway to the Light. If, on the other hand, there is some degree of seduction, anger, addiction or fear within your self-image, then the shadow side of your pathway has emerged. Some sobering choices have to be addressed if you allow addiction to be your guide. If you embrace the Code of the Third Millennium Warrior, you will realize the work necessary for correct action. If ambiguous, call upon honor and courage to bring Light to your decisions.

The awaiting Universe holds the rebirth needed for the newer you. With time and practice the healthier choices in life always bring transformation. Do not fear the Light brought on by these transformations because that is a contradictory concept. Light broadens from the absence of fear. To fear what is good is as insane as the illusion, "Fear of God." God is love and the opposite of fear. Do not allow misinterpretation to deny you of the love that is yours. Continue truth seeking, be patient, and clarity will become more and more pronounced. Clarity will bring prosperity and will lead you to the next level of evolution. This is the evolution of the teacher. The teacher understands growth and sees the reason to ask the next question: "Now that I am growing clearer on my path, **how can I share my experiences with others?**" A journey unto Light always has a value, but if you do not share it, the selfishness of your actions can slow your progress. There is no doubt that "living a good example" is the best illustration of being God-like, but beyond that, all paths will collide with union. Sharing evokes a higher level of the heart's vibration. The vibration of the heart is what expands our universe. Finding your path is no small achievement and finding how to share it becomes yet another magnificent challenge. You may or may not have been surprised by the exercise in the previous lesson. What may surprise you however, is how you can recreate the image of your path (past, present and future) to encompass your vocation simply because **your "Path" becomes a vocation**. Your path is how you go out into the world. It will define how you're perceived and interact just like a vocation. Astrology refers to this as your ascendant. Ultimately, it is safe to say that if your actions support your highest destiny, then you will move forward. If however, your actions do not, then you can slip from your path and lose your way.

The action of the positive or the action of the negative creates a reaction. Refer to your notes concerning the seven descriptions of your Path that you wrote in the previous lesson. Review the past, present and future of your description and reaffirm your story. Look clearly at the life story of your personality and write down three possible vocations that interest you, including the vocation you have at present, for example: mother, store owner, landlord etc.

Possible Vocations

1. _____
2. _____
3. _____

Apply your life's Path from the previous lesson to each vocation. Ask yourself if any of these vocations represent everything described on your path? If they are not in agreement, then inner conflicts can emerge. Inner conflicts occur when you are acting in defiance of your inner priorities (Truth). This can also occur when you are withholding your talents from your present vocation. Have you committed all your talents to your present vocation? If you are not putting forth the true qualities of your path to your vocation, then ask yourself why? Are you really representing your highest self? Do you deny yourself and others of who you really are? Should you be doing something more suited to you or could you do the job better if you applied your true talents? Affect the work; don't let the work affect you.

LESSON THIRTY-SEVEN

Beauty

Within the riches of one's soul lies a chamber of wealth so far reaching it can open doorways to transport power through the universe. Beauty is a gift and a power. It should not be restricted but instead respected for its existence. The fundamental metaphysics of this power is an attraction essence of all that is shared through God's eyes. Whether it is a well-developed physical body, a kind soul or a magnificent sunset, the intrinsic quality of true beauty can become breathtaking even in its unsophisticated state. Physicality is most often associated with beauty simply because we prefer to exist in a physical world. However, the power of beauty is much more far-reaching than material imagery. We must search beyond the surface of outer shells and physical appearance. The physical world is only a fourth of life's journey, and if you live restricted by its boundaries, then you have only started your journey and are not yet free. Those who choose more from life will inherit a higher experience simply by taking their imaginations beyond the one, two, or three-dimensional thinking. Material beauty tends to carry the lust of possession with it, which is why so many people will try to lay claim to externally beautiful things. Passion and desire are human although we must continually be mindful of their shadowy Dragons such as Lust, Greed and Gluttony. Remember you are a work of Art and it is up to you as the artist to define how beautiful you are. The Light Warrior chooses to venture beyond cultural protocol and sees with spiritual eyes. The Light Warrior sees the world like a Raven, being appreciative of the miracles that exist in a daily undertaking. Beauty is the law of attraction. It casts a reflection from the soul to other realms; for example if you project love, people are drawn by their love to the love in you. Vibration has sympathy and attraction is beauty. The soul is your spiritual link to the beauty of the universe, but before you can understand universal beauty we must begin with the inner self. From within we can develop a transmitter/ receiver relationship with esoteric beauty. Once the *connection* is established, the transmitter/ receiver relationship evolves beyond the "me and it" separation. You can then mature to understand true beauty by becoming more truly beautiful. Rather than define a perception of beauty, (after all "Beauty is in the eye of the beholder"), let's imagine looking through the eyes of God as the beholder. It is not difficult to imagine a beautiful landscape or dawn over an ocean, so let's elevate beyond images to the spirituality of beauty. Spirituality is an experience and to grasp the esoteric levels of beauty one must plunge into the experience of God's beauty. Masters of Light (ascended beings) see you only as beautiful; this perplexes the equation because you see yourself as less than you are. Here is where false prophets have convinced you that you are unworthy. False prophets will take advantage of this misunderstanding and force you to live in a false image of your soul. The soul will reach for new highs but you have been taught to discourage such attempts. The false prophet manipulates misinterpretation by attaching a lie to the truth. The truth is beauty is yours; the lie is that you do not deserve it. Attach a truth to a lie and here you find the burden of a lost soul uncertain why we are not being whom we were meant to be. Many people even deny their beauty for fear of what it may attract. Many will unconsciously indulge in overeating, drinking or self-sabotage to diminish the repercussions of what a beautiful person would have to face. The acceptance of beauty is essential, however, there are lessons of ego and vanity that can shadow the process. Vanity is a seduction of beauty and coincidentally unattractive. Because beauty also is a birthright and God's gift, a seductive vanity can tarnish your clarity. Intent is the key. Does your intention to accept your birthrights serve a higher purpose or do you intend to do unnecessary hardship to others with this power? There is nothing wrong with being beautiful but beauty has power and you can do harm with it. Search within yourself for the deeper levels of how you are affected by beauty and how you are affected by seeing yourself as beautiful. It is our responsibility to attach our virtue to our power and create a life that is real and beautiful. This is done by being conscious of other forms of attractiveness beside just your physical appearance. If a physically attractive person will not develop the mind, heart, and soul they will remain out of balance. Security is attained with the balance of your physical, mental, emotional and spiritual self.

Universal beauty is an heirloom to be honored and handed down from one child of God to another. God is beautiful therefore remaining connected to God will convey power. To share this treasure begins an understanding of the transmitter/ receiver relationship. Telepathic communication will ensue this process and the Masters of Light will raise your vibration to channel a higher knowledge. In time, the connection completes, separation dissolves and understanding flows easily. The power of beauty is universal therefore a Truth. Look beyond shallow Truth to experience a real power of attraction. A higher level of your beauty is waiting to be accepted but birthrights must be claimed to be fully mastered. When you are ready, you may be amazed at what you can attract.

Describe how beautiful you are and how you can become even more beautiful.

Physically   _____
                _____

Emotionally   _____
                _____

Mentally   _____
                _____

Spiritually   _____
                _____

Without using blame, what is keeping you from claiming your full potential of beauty?

_____

_____

What would you attract if you embraced your beauty? Are you afraid of what you might attract? Would you feel safe? Do you trust yourself with this kind of power? Have you shut down your powers to be beautiful because of fear, seduction or addiction?

LESSON THIRTY-EIGHT

Honor

In life, we are blessed with bite-size morsels of our true self. We all have tasted what it's like to be who we really are and who we would like to be. This taste can leave a lingering flavor that captures the very essence of our journey. It can also dissipate in the palate, retreating again to the realm of forgotten memory. Every so often we are allowed to dine on this essence of our true self and, for the clear-minded, be reminded who we are. This is not Dying Ground. It is solid ground. Yet, just like Dying Ground, a miraculous moment appears to show you that you have true purpose. Consider it a tease if you will, this taste, this flavor, and this small essence of purpose. It's almost as if the angels have petitioned that you earned a gift of clarity and that perhaps you will find your way home with it. What is unfortunate is how quickly most will allow this gift to slip away like sand through fingers. It takes real courage (a warrior's effort) to reinforce the essence of your real self. Sometimes your life becomes so far removed from who you really are, that a battle is required to fight your way back to a memory. This becomes a test of Honor. **Honorable is he who stands true to himself.** Honor is a spiritual term that breathes power into the hearts of even the darkest soul. What individual would not want to claim this prize we call Honor? But, what is it and how do we claim it? It is a virtue and, like all virtues, we must develop it thoroughly because there can appear to be different levels of discovery. There is Honor to those who live an example of a good life. However, the depth of one's Honor is based on extreme challenge. Yes, it is a warrior's game determined by tests. You see it is not difficult to be kind, giving, and good when life is prosperous and grand. The true challenge comes when we remain true to our highest path while all of life's devastation is crashing down around us. These are the true tests of who you really are. Can you rise above weakness to share your last meal or offer your strength when you have none left? At the bottom of your living hell, can you still be the human being you aspire to be? Are you that strong or are you like most people who would disregard their nobility while slipping backwards into weakness? Inner strength over inner weakness defines the true test of your integrity. **Honor is forged by the example set when hell is on the attack.** It's what you do when you are in a weakened state that defines your worth. How strong will you be when tempted by your greatest seduction? To illustrate a hypothetical example: The lover of a friend attempts to seduce you and you are clearly enraptured. Here is a simple test of Honor. What do you do? Maybe that was too easy. Now let's make it a true test by adding weakness. You are alone and in need of someone's company when this lover of a friend drops by. The magic of chemistry, desire and emotion, along with wine, brings two people face to face with erotic weakness and pleasure. Could you be faithful simply because you gave your word? Are you loyal, dependable, and trustworthy during the difficult times or do you find excuses to justify your weakness? Now we have a pure test of Honor. How well would you do? How well have you done in the past? What if the challenge was about money? What if you gave your word to share and then found a way to take it all? Would you take property that was not yours? Will you break your word and / or find an excuse? These are just a couple of examples in a world filled with abundance and temptation. The world is changing. Some of you will face challenges never before faced and will have to weigh the old standards with the new world. With the old code of Chivalry as well as the Code of the Third Millennium Warrior, your word is your bond. If your word is broken, it is necessary to admit you fell short of yourself. Admitting a shortcoming can help redeem one's honor. People are forgivable because we all are learning. It is human that we fall short of ourselves. These tests allow us to measure our progress. The level that we live within our integrity will determine who we truly are. To be honorable is not easy. It takes practice and discipline. Consider your poor choices from the past and ask yourself if these were tests to determine your value. The weakest points in our lives give opportunity for the greatest gift any warrior could desire. Honor awaits only the few strong enough to **stand true in Battle against the temptations of Darkness.** Thus, **the Acquisition of Honor is the 5th challenge of the Light Warrior.**

LESSON THIRTY-NINE

Victory or Defeat

There is no greater disdain for a Warrior than defeat. The Code of the Third Millennium Warrior proclaims that a Defender of Light cannot be defeated. One cannot defeat a person of pure faith. Defeat is an illusion created by the Culture of the Forgotten Truth to handicap all people with fear. The slightest thought of defeat causes panic in the hearts of millions and can provoke a panic attack. So frightened by this dragon, most people will stop dead in their path and look for other ways to go around it. The Dragon of Defeat is so massive it's difficult to circle and sooner or later must be faced. Defeat is a philosophy that's based on a figment of the Dark side of your imagination. It can be an idea to some and a God to others. Panicked are those who fear defeat. It is amazing when a simple fear-based thought can deny millions the fulfillment of their destinies. Defeat is a great military General and carries much respect in the Dark realm. This single suggestion whispered to the heart, has caused even powerful warriors to miss their mark. However, a Defender of Light does not fear this antagonist because there is a balance to winning and losing. A Defender of Light is a strategist and is able to create a victory from the worst situation. Victory is God's prize to Mankind, but it is up to the clear warrior to uncover it. Darkness will try to claim victory in the presence of defeat, but claiming and achieving are two different things. The words and the experience must merge like religion and spirituality to have real value. If you **believe** (religion) in defeat and accept the **experience** (spirituality) of defeat, then the Dragon will win the day. The Code of the Third Millennium Warrior has no tolerance for this because this is not the true path. Light Warriors expose ignorance with clarity. **If embraced by Light one cannot be**

defeated. There is no defeat because your spirit is still alive. If the heart is pumping, the lungs are breathing and the mind is thinking correctly, there is hope.

Your next exercise is to remember a time when you believed you were defeated. Ask yourself if there was a point when you finally accepted this defeat and moved on. If the answer is yes, try to recall the moment of acceptance. If you answered no, then the illusion of defeat is still haunting the life you live. Acceptance has value, possibly even revelation. Gaining value is a victory. Victory lives beneath the illusion of every defeat. It is up to the warrior to look beneath the illusion of defeat to find the awaiting victory. In the creation of God's children is an empirical formula that gives all children of life the free will to be victorious. No matter what you have been taught by the Culture of the Forgotten Truth we all have the ability to gain what we most need. Ordinarily, what we most need is the development of survival skills. The death of your old life and rebirth into a new way is sometimes necessary for you to overcome a defeated past and survive in destiny's game. This may seem scary, but the cycle must be broken in order to grow and learn. **Maturity is accepting that the person you were must surrender to the person you need to be.** There are parts of your life that are no longer relevant. The past can be a dead vine draining the life out of a tree. Accept it, learn from it, and then lay it to rest. With renewed purpose embark on a mission of faith. This is the way of nature and a way to chart a new course to victory. Accept that the time of past defeats has elapsed. Now claim and snatch victory back from loss. This is the victory of evolution. By accepting that there is knowledge in all experience, see through the fear of defeat into the process underneath. Converting a loss into a win is the mark of a seasoned General and mature warrior. "Pride comes before a fall". Your pride is what forces you to believe that you must always be supreme. Therefore the seduction of supremacy can lead to failure. We all must embrace the role of student at times. It's the humble student that makes the best teacher. There is a prize to be won, when we realize we could have done better. Search for the lesson and its value. Can you fight on? The religion of victory can always overcome the broken religion of defeat. The fear of defeat is manipulated by false prophets to worship a false god. Victory is a religion of recovery with life experience as its salvation. If you believe life is to be experienced, let experience be your victory. Tell your story.

LESSON FORTY

Real / Love

What system of philosophy can or would carry any authenticity without devoting ample respect to the experience of Love? Even a warrior's code would pale in its integrity without embracing this experience. It's said, "Love is the only thing real," and the Code of the Third Millennium Warrior honors this grand and noble wisdom. Unfortunately the English word "Love" is insufficient in its complete scope of all that is the reality of love's experience. For example: God is Love, God is Truth; therefore Love is all things true or real: Honesty, Truth, God, all Love and all real. The alliance of Truth, Love and God exposes the clarity of Light. This manuscript will attempt to analyze intellectually the flavor of what is meant to be tasted. If the essence of our real existence is "Love," then where did the idea come from that we fall in and out of it? Love does not disengage or attach in fleeting moments. Love and Truth is constant, and is therefore just the opposite of the "falling in love" cliché. We are all born of Truth, Creation and Love. At that moment, we are the product of pure non-blocked Love. After a duration in the middle world, being pushed and pulled by heaven and hell, we learn to form layers of fear-based untruth that clouds our memory of divine purity. We do not lose it; we simply forget. By the time of our maturity many layers of reinforced false information have blocked our ability to be loving or real. Then miraculously, someone special comes along to remind us of our source consciousness. We call this "falling in love." "Falling out of Love" is more about finding reasons to justify blocking our emotions so we can choose other alternatives. Judgment and justification seem to play a big role in today's cultural love dance. **Mass illusion creates standards for love and attempts to place love on a social protocol.**

However, illusion (fantasy) without love has no substantial reality. Rules are continually fabricated for that which exists within the creative process. Love is Universal Truth and we all have the ability to be loving beings. It's a part of our empirical formula and more of a natural state than you may believe. Fabricated protocol to control a Universal Truth is a reminder that Darkness would control the boundaries of our talents rather than explore them. The Culture of the Forgotten Truth would have you believe that there must be a reason to love another human being when no reason is necessary. This is as if to say that you need a reason to be a human being. Efforts must be made to regain our source memory of pure Love. This will bring us healing. Choosing a mate is only one special aspect of love fueled with honor and commitment. Finding unconditional Love through commitment (agreed conditions) is a paradox and one of the great mysteries of a committed relationship. **Love has a remarkable ability to tailor itself to any relationship that two people's passion can create.** Hence, relationships like beauty are measured by the level of Love that is either genuine or superficial. The relationship with yourself is also a special aspect of Love. Self-love continues to surface more and more as an antidote for today's complex situations. There are some people that find loving oneself the most difficult challenge and suffer as a result from the Dragon of Inadequacy. These fears manifest layers of blockages that must be removed. Forgiveness is usually the solution for this difficult situation, but forgiveness may require some deep soul recovery. Some people, however, love themselves selfishly and suffer from the Dragon of Vanity. If this is your case scenario, then consider compassion a theater until it, "the act," integrates into your programming. In time, the actor becomes the roll and dialogue. With diligent rehearsals "Loving your neighbor **as** you would Love yourself" can become your reality. Forgiving someone who has wronged you paradoxically requires a warrior's effort. Love has the miraculous ability to manifest the necessary effort and results. The **"Uncovering Love"** strategy is necessary to find forgiveness, healing and freedom. Love is a buried treasure. The deeper you go the more you can find. Uncovering it is difficult in some situations, but letting your heart be your guide can and will eventually lead you to the Justice and the freedom you desire. The heart is alchemy and the Miracle of Light. It is humanity's source essence. It is a gift of unlimited wealth. It expands beyond the boundaries of a single word and it is yours to uncover. The amounts of this gift you choose or how loving you choose to become can only be determined by the limits of your passion and imagination.

LESSON FORTY-ONE

Warriors of the Heart

There are legends of unique individuals who rose above the odds to battle against injustice while exemplifying strength and compassion. Strength and compassion during battle is the paradox of the champions whom we glorify. We are fed fantasies for entertainment, but in reality, where are the real heroes of our generation? Why does the existence of a good-hearted hero intrigue us so? Is it a belief spawned by a memory perhaps? This memory to fight for a noble cause is locked deep within us. It will often uncover who we are and of what we are capable. Now is "the time of the remembering," for the gateway has opened to unlock the once forbidden images of our true self. The Light Warrior spirit is a warrior of clarity, strength and compassion. The Light Warrior possesses a heart open to kindness, full of purpose and pumping with the strength of ten of the warriors who came before. The Third Millennium Warrior will be the clearest of all the ancestors. This warrior will fulfill prophecies pertaining to the battle of Light and Darkness. These are people walking in the shoes of humanitarians. These people are here to aid and protect the values of the human race. It is not important if you can help one person or hundreds, it is only important that you see yourself as the help. Don't ask yourself if you are one of these chosen warriors. This question is a travesty to God's gift of freewill. Instead, ask yourself, "Is this what I choose to be?" Warriors of Light will and must rally to unite against our darkest doomsday prophecies. The Third Millennium Warrior must prepare for this by attaining balance to develop compassion. Rage and destruction are the shadow to the warrior. The Shadowed Warrior now has access to the most powerful weapons in the history of Mankind. The controlling, conquering and uncaring shadow side of the warrior has destroyed much of the beauty this planet had to give us. The Warriors of the Heart are the guiding light that the oncoming generations will need to preserve the earth's beauty and the best of human values. If these warriors of the heart do not step forward, the planet will die. The Lady of the Lake from Arthurian legend will raise the great sword again to be claimed by its true leaders. They will unite the nations. In this age, the lake is a pool of deep truth within the heart. A great sword of mystical light will emerge from the heart for those who have made themselves worthy enough to claim it. Visualize the image to unlock the heart and restore it to its original capacity. Opening the heart is a crucial stage in the training of our future warriors. Claiming and taking hold of your Light is a commitment. Without this power provided by the heart, desolation is the inevitable pathway to our destiny. The Code of the Third Millennium Warrior does not condone a heartless warrior. Heartlessness is a destiny provided by Hell and not that of a Defender of Light. Shape-shift the heart of a warrior and become a **Warrior of the Heart.** Without compassion warriors can never achieve real balance and will inevitably only destroy themselves. It's said, "A man can create an entire city just to rule over it, or a man can destroy an entire city just to rule over it." The choice is clear, and because a warrior's action always carries weight, the destruction or construction of the day is up to you. How do you wish to be remembered: kind, unkind, or not at all? Kindness is rarely forgotten. Search your memory of previous relationships that were kind to you. The heart is a filter that energy passes through and is transformed. It is also easily shut down by fear or emotional pain. The fear of pain is a sultry dragon and snaky to say the least. It can convince you that by shutting down your heart you are protecting yourself from harms way. However, closing your heart shuts down your greatest human potential. Darkness has its own tactical strategies and avoiding pain can seem attractive. If you shut down your heart you may not feel pain, but it's a short-term strategy with a residual long-term effect. Life's lessons are here for you. Denying your lessons will only postpone the work meant to be done. It takes courage to face pain. The longer you delay your life's work, the greater the repercussions. The warrior archetype of the past possessed an iron will, but the Light Warrior must possess an iron faith. Find the courage to deal with your problems now and shelter your loved ones from a destructive future. Pain is a teacher. Pain can teach us compassion, but not if you refuse to feel. Compassion is essential for humanity to endure. **The 6th challenge of the Light Warrior is Compassion.**

LESSON FORTY-TWO

Common Ground

In an age of multi-colored variety and diversity, people more than ever are faced with cultural overlapping. As in a color spectrum, one color overlaps another and a new shade and value is born. It is a natural circumstance to feel at ease with people of like kind, however there is much to be learned from a blend of experiences. In the beginning of every successful relationship an initial effort of similarity is established. **Common Ground is what builds a working language and relationship.** In the student-teacher relationship, the teacher must want to give something and the student must want to accept something. That *want* to exchange defines what is common between the two. On the other hand, if an encounter is less definable, meaning a negative and a positive meet and the differences are in conflict, then the Law of Three requires a neutralizing force. In many cases the neutralizing force may be simple **respect.** Without respect judgment and bigotry can ensue. The concept of bigotry does not support the highest good and is in fact a primary seduction of Darkness. In the end, union is inevitable. Only those with a lack of foresight will argue that we shouldn't unite in a dialogue of peace. The question is, how do we deal with bigotry and how can we merge with those who choose not to blend? Sometimes a reflection is the best choice for difficult relationships. A reflection of honesty, courtesy, strength and respect are good living examples. Living a good example can achieve respect. Asking honest, courteous questions can sometimes lead to a dialogue of hidden information. **Common courtesy** can go a long way to extinguish a prejudiced outcome. Everyone deserves simple human respect. Respect is an easy gift to give; yet it's not a costly gift because it's free. Even an enemy deserves respect before, during and after you neutralize their intentions. With common courtesy even the smallest efforts can prevent the worst outcomes. An acknowledgment of one's dignity is a courtesy. To be ignored can manifest into an insult. Look people in the eyes. This brings strength and dignity to both parties. The Code of the Third Millennium Warrior counsels against false or insincere courtesy. This too can be considered an insult. Never underestimate Honesty. How many times have you heard of a scorned individual offering respect by saying, "At least he was honest"? In time even an enemy can gain forgiveness if his or her sincerity lingers on. It's the people who lie, cheat and deceive that require much more effort to forgive. Everyone has a Dark side, everyone makes mistakes and everyone can be forgiven. We all share a common difficulty forgiving people that wrong us. Even this difficulty is Common Ground.

Perfection lives only in the hearts of those who have no regrets. We all have a higher purpose and we are all evolving into a spiritual union of Light. Even a dark soul can turn around and move to the Light. All that is important is to recognize that you are not the only one on this journey. The completion of your path relies on a united effort. People will continue to communicate with their ideas, their hearts and their hands. It takes the evolved person to extend communication into the spiritual realms. When the final leap of faith is made, there will no longer be a priority to build a world that relies on spiritual separation. Without separation we live in compassion, not judgment, respect not contempt, and tolerance not condemnation. **Judgment comes from me looking at you and seeing my dislikes in your behavior.** Being aware of flaws is not enough. The evolved people are those awake and doing the work. If we can see flaws in others, then why can't we see our most common desire to be respected? Finding Common Ground is a primary aspect of everyone's journey. We must realize and accept that we share similar difficulties understanding relationships. Our difficulties as well as our pleasures can unite us. "Ashta Ha" is a Native American phrase meaning *"I am you looking at me seeing who I am."* Everyone offers us an opportunity to view our reflections. See yourself in everyone you meet. The purpose of life is relationships. All relationships have information; some may seem insignificant and some monumental. Life begins from a relationship between hosts or parents. In many ways you grow to be that parent; you are your mother and your father, yet you are still uniquely you. There is a part of our parents that exists in us and us in them. Sometimes it is difficult to recognize the quality of these relationships, yet denial will only ignore source data. **Denial is a magic created by Darkness to induce blindness.** It is so easy to deny or place blame on the parents. This can work but is only a temporary strategy. At some point, placing blame will only manifest the virus of victimization and delay your true purpose. Your highest quest may have begun in your parental self. You may even carry the very challenge for victory that your parents were unable to complete. Ask yourself, "What is it that my parents wanted most and may never have achieved?" You must ask this with a detached perspective, remembering to keep it simple. Most lifelong quests are so simple they are completely passed over. Simple, common respect may be the very desire that has been so elusive. Self-worth, love, recognition, power, peace, knowledge, courage or any of a thousand invisible victories may have been shrouded by a parent's fear, seductions or what you see as their flaws. You must go beyond the concept of wealth to the true emotions and find the soul of the person in question. If you can do this without passing judgment, the answers you find may surprise you. Think back on what is the very **basic** desire your parents wanted more than anything. Why did they want these things? Name three wants that motivated them above all else and write them down. Keep each to a one-word answer.

1._____ 2._____ 3._____

What is common among the three wants of your parents and you? This type of source research can be helpful to recognize one's own personal past, present and future. Please note this exercise does not work under the influence of judgment, blame, or victimization.

It is not a coincidence that people tend to mimic their mother or father, as they get older. Lineage has memory and the gateway to ancestral memory is in all of us. Those who never met their biological parents must accept that these people gave you all that you needed and nothing more. If your relationship with your mother or father is more detached than attached, then remember, you are a child of God and creation of nature; therefore, you are partly the creator and the creation. We are both. To become a powerful individual, it is important to go our own way. Anyone can find personal success on their own, but we will only find fulfillment if we are able to overcome separation to find each other.

LESSON FORTY-THREE

Male/Female

The idea that Men are one thing and Women are something else seems to be the easiest solution to simplify the difficult equations of today's relationships. However, a man is a human being first and then he is a man; a woman is a human being first and then she is a woman. Problems arise not as much from our differences, but from the inability to remember: What is a human being? **Being human exemplifies why men and women are allies for a great cause and adversaries for a poor one.** The Culture of the Forgotten Truth will sell you a story that men and women are from different planets. This debate at times seems playful, but debate of this issue manifests separation and complicates the faith that oneness is possible. The two are not aliens from different planets but instead a force assembled here to save this planet. What the Culture of the Forgotten Truth has denied to teach is while it is easier and sometimes fashionable to be judgmental, it requires the essence of being human to be tolerant. Though it is fashionable to contrast men and women, it is inaccurate to label their supposed differences as Truth. It is more truthful to say that the cultural protocol for each gender was seemingly written in two different worlds. Men and women both are dichotomies created with varying amounts of masculine and feminine energy. Evolution proves the obvious: men can sensitize and women can empower. This seems like common sense, and yet we perpetuate separation whenever possible. The bigger picture is about the gentle balance of masculine and feminine energy. This balance of nature is what balances our humanity. However, differences are clearly defined in our culture to create separation with subtle dogma. This is an exercise in social bigotry.

What would convince you that you've been betrayed by

your own cultural protocol? To insult your way of thinking is undoubtedly a delicate matter not to be taken lightly without some sensitivity. Sensitivity is a core element of understanding and perhaps the initial step we should take together toward awareness. When questioning someone's system of belief, the inability to remain sensitive can lead to unnecessary conflict. A lack of sensitivity can undermine even the best of intentions. This culture wants you to believe that a sensitive person is not a warrior. This is not true. The Warrior of the Heart (Light Warrior) cannot be achieved without sensitivity. You've been programmed to associate sensitivity with femininity and with weakness. Femininity, however, is not weakness and neither is an **acute intuitive awareness**. To speak one's heart defines honesty; to express one's heart defines artistry; and yet, if a man feels his heart openly he is culturally termed "weak." Striving and achieving one's goals is described as successful and even ambitious, but if a woman asserts herself above the culture's parameters then she is labeled offensively. These observations are two examples of how our culture has forgotten the truth and is being slowly reminded. Gender distinctions create dissension and split the Army of Light in half. Both men and women are enslaved by these false separations. Our culture wants you to believe we are two separate species. The empowered woman and the sensitive man are looked upon as mutants of our society. Our culture programs us to believe that the feeling man is not a *real* man and that the aggressive woman is other than a *real* woman, but real strength and understanding lies in developing balance. Evolution is tolerating individuality. Men and women are evolving by learning from each other. The design of men and women is a universal schematic. This design is the perfect layout for the student-teacher relationship in its most classical form. If the idea were accepted that **men and women are not opposing but instead composing**, we could realize that we have been both student and teacher to each other since the beginning of time. Both men and women possess the same spiritual birthrights. Both share the Warrior birthright as well as the birthrights of beauty. Though we may choose different methods of expression, both gifts are in no way exclusive.

Men and women can exist as allies and this is how it was meant to be. However, first we must ally in the goal to not have men and women opposing each other. Just as our culture pits one brother against another because of simple differences, it also creates sexist bigotry. Bigotry is the hiding of all similarities in Darkness while exposing only contrast so that blame and judgment may form. The power of the word dictates "as above so below." To voice bigotry is the definition of a bigot. To choose bigotry no matter how harmless it may seem is a seduction. Bigotry is the shadow side of religion and a Dragon of fierce repercussions. This Dragon attaches a truth to a lie and creates a level of shallow truth and false reality. One true statement added to an inspired hypothetical situation can make for a convincing argument. It is a deceptive magic that can transform fear and ignorance into an idea that seemingly makes sense. It takes the power of the Correct Question to break through the surface of shallow truth into the pool of deep truth. It takes a Defender of Light to stand against false propaganda. Splitting people because the culture dictates it is a prime example of how many are seduced by Darkness and deception. Keeping the truth buried is a clear and decisive Strategy of Darkness. To dwell on separation is a disconnected religion.

"We hold these truths to be self-evident, that all men are created equal, that they are endowed by their Creator with certain unalienable rights, that among these are life, liberty, and the pursuit of happiness."

THE DECLARATION OF INDEPENDENCE, JULY 4, 1776

All men are created equally **from the feminine**, but unfortunately our culture indoctrinates inequalities almost immediately after birth. We are taught propaganda concerning what men and women are allowed to accomplish in our lifetimes. We teach our children to have the girl experience or the boy experience, the black, the white, the rich and the poor experience.

The Masculine and the Feminine combined generate a powerful creative force. Creation is an act of God like power. The Creation of children is the united experience. Simplicity is the example set by nature. Complexity is how we redefine nature. Still to this day we read countless publications of male and female protocol filled with shallow truth cloaked with bigotry and falsehoods. Except for basic biological traits, the behavioral arguments really do not apply to every person. People seek ways to find differences. How much of the information have you really questioned, or do you, like most people, feed on the differences? Perpetuating and finding fault in our differences only creates segregation. It always requires more work to bridge the gap between two uncommon perspectives. Is it not true that even the biological differences seem to suggest that the union of the two creates oneness? Is it not true that the union of the two perpetuates creation? Most people find it easier to allow separation rather than fight for unity.

Gender equality is a difficult concept to totally agree on, as it is opposite from our cultural mandate. For the most part, we merely emulate nothing more than our own cultural protocol (sleep-walking zombies). Perhaps it is only the rules that we have accepted for men and women that create these different perspectives. Men and women share many different types of life experiences and, as a result, can sometimes see different perspectives on a similar issue, but is it not wisdom to understand all interpretations of an issue? Education is how the human race evolves. Today's men will be as sensitive as their cultural protocol will allow them to be. Today's women will be as forceful as is necessary within the boundaries of cultural protocol. **Evolution demands** the dismissal of this segregated nonsense and out-dated cultural protocol based on separation. A Warrior of the Heart possesses the masculine (conquering) abilities with the feminine (surrendering) abilities, thus creating a balanced and empowered individual who understands the value of both strategies. Men and Women, empowered as allies, are the resources to do what ever needs to be done. If you're uncertain what that is, consider this idea: Almost everyone sees themselves as "a good person," but in actuality very few people have the discipline to be "a good person." Can you embody **strength** as well as **compassion**; the masculine combined with the feminine? If so, you have broken down cultural oppression and freed yourself from misguided stereotyped limitations. Relationships are extremely perplexing for the conqueror unable to surrender or the surrendered unable to conquer. It is so much easier to just blame a failed relationship on the other person. Placing blame separates us all, but the Culture of the Forgotten Truth would not have it any other way. To move beyond this social dogma will take both the feminine and the masculine within us. It will take our strength to pursue the Truth and our sensitivity to understand and accept it. The Army of Light is composed of a unified force. This may seem like an impossible dream if you allow differences to control you. However, the Light Warrior is bred to overcome the impossible.

LESSON FORTY-FOUR

Respect

The highest natural courtesy life can bestow upon life is the virtue of Respect. In nature this virtue is a constant. When the boundaries of respect break down, the balance of nature will create havoc to restore that balance. It is a simple concept, yet it proposes the most elusive challenge for many people. It would seem that respecting each other would fall within the boundaries of common sense but it does not. Animals less evolved naturally partake in this ritual. Yet, people must be rigorously reminded of rules such as, "Do unto others as you would have them do unto you or Love thy neighbor as you Love thyself." It is a common practice to lose respect for someone we don't approve. We tend to devalue opinions other than our own. Two opposing opinions can meet in conflict as if on a battlefield. In accordance with the law of threes, the positive and the negative can be neutralized with a balancing force. The neutralizing force is achieved in most personal relationships through respect. If two opposing forces disagree, a settlement, or at least an acceptance, can normally be found if respect is maintained. The idea unfortunately can get lost sometimes, especially for those who pride themselves in being right. This is why a lack of respect leads the ignorant down the corridors of judgment and denial. It is common that people will disrespect others to gain superiority for themselves. **Respect should be deserved, more so than demanded.** Demanding it only perpetuates laziness. Earning it offers a course of action on display as a living example. In most cases a good example will earn people's respect. Mutual regard creates balance. You must give to receive. Listen first to opposing views because it is courteous. Be mindful of where the information is coming. Does the information have any merit at all? If you can find a place of common ground a dialogue is possible. Being disrespectful is met with opposition and eventual chaos. Everyone has an individual reality. Honoring each other defines "The Dream" and vision of a King's clarity. Creating "The Dream" into reality is the work of a warrior poet.

Respect requires a simple honest gesture perpetuated with a kind heart. Being polite is humility. A lesson in humility is a lesson in respect. God gives us the respect to have our own choice and go our own way. Clearly mankind doesn't always follow the higher path, but we have still been given the courtesy to do as we see fit. To look at our brother, disagree, respect his wishes, and allow him his choices displays God-like temperament. It is rarely considered that God is Humility, but it's true. There is much disaster in this world because God has trusted people to go their own way. Imagine, though, if we deserved no respect from God. We would no longer have a choice. What if God had no trust in people? When we lose trust in each other, and disrespect someone else's rights, religion, family, race, or life style, we shift away from light. Light is clarity through God's eyes. Communication breaks down when you place yourself in a position that denies someone his or her free will. By disrespecting a person's free will, dialogue again ventures down the dark corridors of judgment and separation. We must put faith and effort into the belief that humility will one day find those who show disrespect to good people. There are many ways to deny God's work. Cheating a person's free-will by manipulating them with guilt, anger or violence for selfish reasons is intimidation. If someone chooses to travel a different path or prefers privacy, as long as they don't break laws or harm others, we should respect it. If someone reaches out with kindness, reciprocate it, because they are showing you as a human being, proper respect. Sometimes we forget courtesy and sometimes we even disrespect ourselves. Sometimes we forget our bodies in our search for fulfillment. As a result we end up dragging our body through the process.

Our body is the vessel needed to convey and transport our lower, middle, and higher self. If we do not take care of it we will never completely be respecting ourselves. Respect is a virtue and a Truth in the world today. Our planet and her position deserve the utmost respect. Thoughtfulness for the earth, wild life, other people and ourselves must be practiced. A Defender of Light must develop compassion for all living things so that all living things will offer respect in return. **Respecting All Life (Humility) is the 7th challenge of the Light Warrior.**

LESSON FORTY-FIVE

Creative Alliance

The Creative Alliance between God and people forms the Gateway into our spiritual world. This concept begins with imagination. There is no human being who has developed a relationship with God that has not tapped their imagination to do so (the leap of faith). It is also equally clear that there is no human being who has developed a relationship with another person that has not tapped his or her imagination. The union of your imagination with another is the divine imagination of a Creative Alliance. There is much power and accomplishment that can be channeled through a Creative Alliance. There are many extraordinary results that are possible once a person accepts the God-gift to create. Accepting a God-gift is a choice that is yours alone. You could choose to be an extraordinary person doing ordinary things or an ordinary person doing extraordinary things. Being fully immersed in your ability to create is the key to stepping into your power and becoming an extraordinary person doing extraordinary things. Creative ability, however, must be exercised and developed and is not exclusive to the spiritual world. The mental, physical and emotional worlds also require creating or recreating. To mentally seek and experience inspiration and then to express physically your passion is what makes a person extraordinary. The Creative Alliance of the mental, spiritual, emotional and physical in balance is the essence of real human power. Apply this balance fashioned in the image of a kind heart and you will find the key that unlocks the door to true divine greatness. You have the ability to create love, kindness, and compassion in the image of you. This is not an easy task. It requires effort, honesty, courage and listening. The courage to listen to honesty takes serious effort sometimes. Many questions will arise. Are we created in the divine image as a microcosm of God, or are we vehicles of God's will? It is a noted debate to separate divine inspiration into these two perspectives. First, let's take revelation, the voice of creation and the creative process. The Creator is creation and therefore creative. Now comes the debate: Is God creating through man as a vehicle or is man emulating God by creating? Are we being moved or are we doing the moving? Perhaps it is simply both. However, this much is certain: all processes that pass through people will be flavored by our own personal imperfections. The question that arises with channeling information is if we are expressing God's will, are we relaying accurately or are we interpreting it in our human image? Where does divinity end and interpretation begin? Is God coming through us or are we reaching out and expressing ourselves in the image of our illusions? Why is it that one person's expression of God's will can be loving and another maliciously violent? It is not the concern of the Code of the Third Millennium Warrior to debate who is right or wrong. The challenge is to move mentality from "My Light is Right" to a united "Light for Right". A united simplistic alliance of spiritual Light here on earth is the Light Warrior quest. When religions unite for a common plan of good, then a Creative Alliance and Army of Light will emerge. All expression of God's will is flavored by the imperfections in the human character. Imperfection is the initial common ground that all races and religions share. Human flaws are a primary focus of the truth seeker. The Code of the Third Millennium Warrior's intention is not to recreate you as perfect, but more so to recreate you forgiving, which neutralizes judged imperfections. Taking you back to your source essence of humanity does this. The less God's will is tainted by our character flaws, the purer our visions and the kinder our expression. All one needs to do is witness a sunrise over the ocean to understand a peaceful sense of clarity. Creativity is a powerful God-Gift and has its Darker side. Be careful not to create negatively. Clearly all people have this potential. The fact is that there are numerous avenues to achieve greatness and each one of us must make the attempt our own unique way. Begin internally and then bring it forward. Sharing our talent is important. You may believe that what you know cannot be taught, but all knowledge can be taught; it just may be difficult for the student to hear. This is why creating a language that can be heard is first necessary. **"A Creative Alliance between race, religion, creed and gender must be found. Create this Circle of Light and you will be an inspiration and teacher for us all."** This statement is the essence of the Light Warrior way.

LESSON FORTY-SIX

God is Creative

The game is life. The game was created for **Children** to create. Life is creation. Creation is **God** and God is the Creator. Together we find connection through the **Spirit** of Creativity. **God, Child** and **Spirit** are sacred. Artistic inspiration is the passion of energy. Through the spirit anything is possible. The journey to find God, to find Truth, to find Light is your creative process. Like the artist who crafts a work of art, you are the creator of your world. Each day begins with the world you construct. Each day ends with the world you've constructed. Building a catwalk to find God is the spiritual journey. The artist is you and you are the art. All things are possible if you are able and willing to inspire your imagination. Choose to stay in the process and not to stay in bed. Step out into the great world and use your imagination to determine the size of your universe. God is Creative, so why would anyone choose not to be? To build a good life is to mimic divine architecture. "Creativity is the highest form of human intelligence." Science will never prove all the possibilities provided by the inventive mind. The distance between the scientific and the creative is the distance between people and God. The two must integrate so as not to be separate. If you cannot appreciate your imagination, then you have not discovered your true potential. Even beyond the image of your highest self is a world of uncharted originality. In these uncharted waters exists a sleeping ocean of reality waiting for a time to be remembered. With a single leap of faith, imagine the possibility and power open to you alone. Every individual journey will at some point rely on a leap of faith. Have you made it, or are you still waiting? To unite spiritual concepts requires a giant leap of faith. It will happen, but first we must stand in our power, transcend above and beyond the limitations of our narrow thinking. Standing in your power will mean exploring new ways to be greater than you were yesterday. You may find both self and selflessness within you. This may seem contradictory, but in fact it is a healthy self-image. If your present condition in life feels unhealthy, recreate your self anew. You are birthed from creation and you can deliver a rebirth. Free will is the divine gift of expression. **Free will is complete creative freedom.** It sounds simplistic, but there is much work to be done removing fear barriers and deep ingrained negative patterns. These barriers exist because we accidentally sculpted them. The alternative to a poorly sculpted life is the life of your dreams. Restructure yourself from the heart and the alchemy will complete you. Take the best of who you want to be and become whom you want to be. The three reasons why we feel unfulfilled are that we **chose poorly and missed**, we have not **followed through,** or we just **haven't decided** what we want. It is easy to quit; therefore, **the Warrior Spirit must be merged with the Spirituality.** This process is the awakening of the Light Warrior. You alone have the talent to shape a better life. Only you can remember your highest virtues. Being other than yourself is the sacrificial path and the religion of a sheep, not the Way of the Lion. Mold yourself into an archetype of what is important based on what you can control. Seek out your true virtues, not your superficial desires. Status only has value when measuring the compassion in your heart.

Imagination is a God-gift and has a seductive Dark side. Wouldn't you rather have no imagination at all than to have it destroy you? Use your imagination well to develop a life that is magnificent. Free expression gives you the power to apply your imagination to life. Take who you are, build a better person, and then build the world that you require to support that image. Share your gifts with others. This is the definition of power, this is the power of Creation, and this is the power of the Creator.

Gateway through the stars:
Using your imagination for meditation

Visualize the heavens, stars and space in your mind. See the stars move together to create a tunnel. See through your mind's eye as you pass through a tunnel of light. Stay with the tunnel as it twists and turns through space and time. Experience your image being transported through space. The tunnel will take you to an open space filled with light. Focus on being centered and staying in the moment. In a room filled with light, open yourself to converse with an Ancient being. Here in this place remain respectful. Greet a counsel of one who should be honored as a Master of Light. Say hello to your higher self.

LESSON FORTY-SEVEN

The Gateway

Since the last of the Wizards vanished centuries ago, the earth was left to us, the students of life. This is a crude reality for the earth and mother of us all, but a reality she had to accept. With the constructive destruction of trial and error, we have forged a faint image of ourselves left behind from a distant memory. More and more we continue to remember, and as a result we develop technology for documenting experience and communicating it with one another. We are growing closer to the clarity of unification that we've so unconsciously desired. This unconscious memory to document and communicate is the program that has delivered us to the brink of the Gateway. The Gateway was referred to in ancient text as Babylon (Gateway of God). Ancient text offers many mysteries to the curious adventurer on a virtuous quest. As a result an open heart unlocked the gateway, allowing both the Masters of Light and students of life to take their rightful places together. A teacher longs to teach, but only to willing students. Masters of Light fight to find their vessels and return. We must also fight to meet them halfway. The distance between point A (the opening) and point B (the arrival) is the distance of who we were and who we are becoming. This distance between point A and point B has time collapsing and point B is becoming a reality. It takes courage to pass through the Gateway and will take warriors to embrace the changes. The ascended Master's are willing to communicate to those who will listen. As students of life we are here to document all experience with words. The words create languages, the languages create common ground and the understanding of each other's language is growing. Language will become one as with religion. It is the memory that **all things are one** that has created this possibility. The universe's language is speaking to us. However, **you stand alone in your responsibility to listen. It is up to you.** Our separation between physicality and spirit keeps us in servitude but it is our compassion that has unlocked the Gateway. On the other side of the Gateway is a dimension of spirit offering knowledge beyond the physical reality. It is here at the doorway that student and teacher meet.

Perhaps it would be best to give an example of what it would be like to see us from the other side of another dimension. Imagine yourself standing at the doorway of your home. The door is now open and you see a guest on your porch. The guest is a perceived lesser being, let's say a wolf. The wolf is uncertain if it is safe. You are uncertain if it is safe to allow him to enter. You are certain you are superior to a wolf; after all, you are a civilized human being. However, the wolf has found its way to your door. He has even scratched on your door long enough to get you to open it. Now what? Well, first you question, **should I close the door or let him inside?** You assess the wolf for information. Eventually if you trust it is safe you **might let him enter.** It will inevitably come down to this: a perceived fear and anger will keep him out, while a perceived trust and kindness will allow him inside. **The Gateway is no different.** "It is only the virtuous knight that can find the Holy Grail."

Now consider the perceptions of the wolf. The wolf gazes at a human for the first time; because the wolf is still young, he is curious. He assesses the human looking down on him and feels compelled to explore. He sniffs at the doorway to see if he is safe and wonders what is the best choice. He could run, but doesn't. He could attack but is uncertain. The door might close or the conflict might put him in worse position than he is in now. He could open his heart, show affection, and be respectful and loving. Maybe not, the human might perceive weakness and after all a wolf is capable of fierce attack. The human and the wolf stand there at the doorway. Oddly the two, student and teacher, mirror each other's jesters in an attempt to create a language.

Perhaps one day the wolf may decide to drop his self-importance, possibly even, drop his fear and aggression. Perhaps one day the wolf will, through a leap of faith, have the courage to walk in the door lovingly and respectfully. The Code of the Third Millennium Warrior requests you to take a leap of faith, become the wolf *without fear or aggression* and walk respectfully and lovingly through the gateway into a growing concept of a united spirituality.

LESSON FORTY-EIGHT

Faith

There is no grander inspiration than someone who completely believes in victory. The Code of the Third Millennium Warrior is designed to open a door to activate this great belief. Therefore ingrained is the intent to trust, challenge and win victory. In this great belief, honesty is victory and the truth is more powerful than a lie. Persuading you to trust that there is a real destiny is one objective to creating Faith. Persuading you to believe that your destiny coincides with the path of all of us, as well as your ancestors, presents another challenge in Faith. Fear of the unknown is by far the most difficult fear to overcome. It can take you off balance and off your path. To neutralize the unknown fears we have the power of Faith.

Unlocking the unknown ancestral memory is relevant to an authentic journey. The complications of today's generations have brought many distractions and as a result people have lost their ancient memories. These are the memories that can lead a wanderer home. Together, we will continue to unlock the mysteries of who we are. As a result, you will also uncover along the way the rights you possess and the rights you've squandered. Life is full of lessons learned and past life memory is a treasure of learned information. It can unfold a more simplistic time of understanding. The Culture of the Forgotten Truth would diminish your faith in what is real by convincing you that there is another protocol to follow. Then it tries to sell you on sensations that can cheat your very soul. You are meant to do great things and yet you're living the life of someone else. How is this possible? Somehow everyone receives clues to who they were meant to be, so why do we choose to listen to a different voice? The Culture of the Forgotten Truth speaks loudly with its fear and drowns out the purity of the real voice. Have faith in the real voice because we have denied our heart felt virtue by accepting cultural misdirection. We have allowed unhealthy people to create an unhealthy future. As a result, we have denied the enlightened path, guided by respectful angels. Instead most people choose a lesser path guided by pushy and convincing lost souls. Believe it or not, it isn't a required task to unlock your mind and listen to the real voice within you. Most people choose to remain deaf. Do you listen to your heart? If you do not trust your heart, then the odds grow stronger against you. Faith is all a matter of confidence. Faith can rock the darkest floor of the underworld's foundation. Faith is a powerful weapon in a warrior's arsenal. No fighter has ever won a real victory without it. To believe in the highest due process is to empower with auxiliary fuel. As long as you have Faith you cannot be defeated because there is hope. This is a free-will choice; however, much of one's faith is determined far beyond your ability to choose. Great Faith or the lack thereof is handed down as if a family heirloom. Ancestral memory is based largely on ancestral belief. This is not a call to blame the past, but is instead simply knowledge to accept and redirect now. The great council of your ancestral bloodline sits together in the hopes that you will recognize that what is common in all of us is in your heart. Again, there is a shadow side of this gift. Faith turned negative can open the door to all the dragons of the shadow world. Negative belief occurs when Darkness has turned your strength against you. Turning your creativity against yourself is the Art of Sabotage. Sabotage keeps you stuck with no certain direction. If your life is stuck, begin by looking at your Faith supply. Is the supply positive or victimized? It is appropriate also that ancestral guidance be summoned to support and defend your battles at hand. Having faith in yourself and your family begins the opening dialogue that will assemble the spiritual clan for counsel. Together with you and assisting you, your family can ally to make you stronger. This may seem unlikely to the pragmatic, but with faith even the impossible becomes attainable. DNA transference is a scientific fact. If your physical, mental and emotional traits are transferred through DNA, then why not a spiritual transference? Will this idea ever be proven? Maybe, but proof is only necessary when Faith is slipping. Trust that God is speaking through your heart. Allow the real voice to guide you. You will know what is right. If not, use all your resources to get back to the heart. If the heart is directing you to gather more information, ask yourself, "What would the highest image of myself do?" The opportunities will present themselves. Above all, you must believe in yourself. **Faith is the 8th challenge of the Light Warrior.**

LESSON FORTY-NINE

Fire and Light

Fighting without fear or anger

Most People believe that anger is necessary to fight, but this is a distortion of the truth. It takes true clarity to distinguish between an angry expression and an expression of serious and passionate intent. The question to this lesson is, "Is it possible to move into conflict and never unleash the Dragon of Anger?" *Herein lives the challenge, training and mystery of a spiritual warrior.* To move into aggression **with anger** or fear feeds the Dark spiritual dragons. Virtue is what casts out our demons. So how does one fight with serious intent and keep a pure heart? To voice the soul's truth may be your only reprieve to release the havoc of an angry dragon trapped inside. Since there is no English word to describe healthy anger, it is usually termed as **passion.** Acting out with aggressive intent for a higher cause, such as Justice, or survival, or something constructive is you igniting your warrior flame. As you know fire can keep us alive when cold and can destroy when left uncontrolled. Misinterpretation of a warrior's fire is a very delicate matter. *The pools of blood run deep in our history from the ignorant that misinterpret the message of Light.* Darkness can easily seduce the "holier than thou." The righteous can be judgmental and not guided by the heart. This is the Red Dragon disguising itself as clean when it is not. It takes the careful perception of a clear and grounded individual to determine the difference. A sheep will blindly follow those who use aggressive deceptive tactics, but the Lion chooses a different path. The Lion will attack with forceful intent, but without malice. A Lion is simply being a creature of nature ready to protect, defend and survive. The Light Warrior is a Lion empowered by virtue. It is good and healthy to exercise the warrior spirit as long as you do it with your anger in check. Checking your anger takes practice and discipline. Get to know your internal and external enemies. Staying grounded and protected by light can fend off an illusive attack from a negatively driven force. Staying centered while your opponent is angry allows you the opportunity to combat the attack, possibly with neutralization. Neutralization is a higher level of war practiced by the Peacemakers. As it is possible that sometimes a twist of fate can place you in bad company, a Defender Of Light must stand up for what is clear. This is the power, courage and individuality of the Light Warrior Spirit. It is not an easy task to step outside of destructive anger. There is never anything easy about anger at all. It can feed on you internally and manifest externally in the blink of an eye. Staying strong when everyone else is losing their humanity to anger and fear will be the challenge of the Light Warrior and your moment of truth. Changing times will rock the face of humanity and you may be called upon as a Light Warrior to represent your core convictions. The passion of your core convictions will determine your message and place in the game. Fighters must learn the skill necessary to fight without anger, malice or fear. This is not a skill taught by the Culture of the Forgotten Truth. You must train yourself to be affective and powerful yet clear minded and calm. You must train yourself to be lethal and yet sensitive to the value of your humanity. It is the best-trained athlete that is the most sensitive to his or her body's potential. Have you ever felt the need to fight without the need to destroy? The passion of your convictions is the driving force to bringing imagination to life. Passion without anger is the key to unleashing the Light Warrior Spirit into the game. Removing anger from your intent is not easy and requires a strong **commitment to non-violence.** This commitment will separate the Warriors of Light from the destructive Warrior Shadow. It is stress and anger that exposes the destruction of the warrior flame. The angry warrior is far more common than the Light Warrior and why many regard the warrior concept only as destructive. Anger is illusive and you must have outlets to release the anger in you. You must challenge your anger with tolerance. You must challenge your fear with courage. Apply your energy to transforming anger into something constructively passionate. For those who are tormented with violent anger, transforming your anger should become a religion for salvation. Violent people must learn the severity of their actions. Extreme cases will require assistance and training methods to express or release anger. It can be channeled. You must exercise the body to release the anger that is already trapped. Although you may see yourself as a warrior, if angry, you have only been seduced by the shadowy seductions of fire and tap a small potential of your true power.

LESSON FIFTY

Revenge

Now we come to the essence of shadow, the most deeply contaminated aspect of the human heart. In the midst of finding our true self we find behind the darkest door lingers a blood lust. Here in the belly of the beast lives a festering, menacing life force that offers a viciousness to mirror the ugly within us. This ugliness is the darkest side of our heart because it is genuine passion gone insane. **Revenge,** once called, "A dish best served cold," is by far as dangerous a dragon to slay as any fear we face. While **vengeful,** the power of the human heart no longer beats for love, but instead is blocked with its energy rerouted through a chamber of vile intention. Revenge is black magic evil that can mystically infest your heart. This is why Revenge is a spiritual virus that directly attacks emotions and can outbreak into a crime of unholy passion. Once it has settled in the heart it is always a struggle to maintain your highest self. Even a simple courtesy becomes painstakingly difficult to bring into being. Revenge strokes our most primal desires because we all have a primal and inherited need to win. It will delude you with the illusion of happy outcomes and can persuade you that payback is justifiable behavior. Here is where all the faces of the Dragon come together and work in unison. Pride, anger, lust, greed, sloth, fear, deceit, envy and gluttony creep forward behind the masquerade of self-proclaimed justice and fair play. Revenge is a Master of Darkness and the Masters of Light must be called upon to ally with your remaining noble self. Make no mistake about it, when acting on the corruption of Retribution you have shut down the kindness in your heart, and no longer personify what is good in the human spirit. However, there are options available to the warriors that are Defenders of Light. These options are strategic in action and allow a reprieve. It is a difficult challenge and requires discipline and a tight reign on corrupted emotions. The stages of salvation are **(1) The Request, (2) The Detachment, (3) The Alternative** and **(4) The Act.** The work is not easy. You may not believe it while in a vengeful state, but forgiveness is the kindest thing you can do for yourself.

The Request: First, to overcome revenge is a huge challenge that will require as much assistance as possible. Through conversation, prayer or meditation, call upon all possible aid that can benefit you, for example: family, friends, teachers, guides, and all emotional and spiritual support.

The Detachment: Second, accept that through Revenge the heart becomes corrupted; therefore a cleansing is necessary. This is the sole purpose for your spiritual support. *Requesting, on any spiritual level, the destruction to come to another human being is the definition of Black Magic and can open your spiritual world to real evil.* The goal is to detach from the pride or anger that has invaded your emotions so that the clarity and kindness in the heart can reclaim and free your soul. This may also require you to work your body.

The Alternative: Third is the opposite of where darkness has taken you. This is a pure act of love. It's said, "The best revenge is living well," and this serves beautifully as an example of self-love. Be kind to yourself. Do what makes you feel good. Redirect your energy from retribution to a constructive emotional self-indulgence. Search for that act of love elsewhere, which may in some way reclaim your heart and help you to move on. In some cases, perhaps not immediately, an act of purity may teach a higher lesson that will be remembered. Reclaiming your heart can even change the course of events that has broken down the relationship. Be honest and true to your higher self. This is the beauty the heart requires. Love offers many roads to correct a situation. The journey is finding one. The heart is the vehicle for alchemy and can transform the victim into a Light Warrior. Try to focus beyond the blame. Vengeance is simply the dark side of the heart stuck and needing empathy. Focus on freedom. Darkness into Light is turning our dragons into a gracefully productive dragonfly. Perhaps finding a different way of loving will help. Find out what your lessons are in this relationship, so as not to repeat them. It's been said, "Our enemies make our greatest teachers."

The Act: Ease into motion with graceful intention. Grace will lead you away from vengeance. Graceful movement is important. Easy, patient and graceful is *The Act* and the action toward forgiveness. Healing the heart and learning the lesson is the only victory discernible from Revenge.

LESSON FIFTY-ONE

Forgiveness

"Misfortune is a human condition; without misfortune we would not be human." This is a Taoist concept and should be respected as wisdom. Misfortune surfaces in everyone's life but in no way is it the ruler of our domain. A warrior is the master of one's own destiny. Many believe that misfortune is the repercussion from a type of debt known as Karma. Karma is a valid argument and one that will be debated till the end of time. Good-Karma, bad-Karma and the ongoing struggle to pay past debts is a widely practiced system of thought. Understandably, this can work in your favor as good fortune does shine on those who live a virtuous life. In the end Karma becomes the balance left from paying debt, which leaves an oppression to be concluded in the next life. The Webster's definition of debt is a sin. To live in debt is an oppression that declares war against freedom. Many people live their entire lives in debt and so this concept of debt paying has become normal. Even the insanity of abuse can become normality over a period of time. The Culture of the Forgotten Truth uses debt to enslave and control people. If Karmic debt liberates you from darkness, then the Code of the Third Millennium Warrior supports your beliefs. However, if you are locked in the belief that Karmic debt paying is the only way to justify your punishment, then supersede this with a lesson in Forgiveness. Warriors must take responsibility for their actions, access the damage, do the maximum that can be done, and then move on. Forgiveness is the great freer of our souls and the freer of Karmic debt. No life is locked in an unchangeable Karmic pattern despite what you have been told. People talk into the idea of living many lifetimes; however, we have lived many different lives in this lifetime. **Good fortune supports those who change**

their life to fulfill their destiny. It is fear and seduction that would persuade you to stay on a path that is not working because of an enormous debt. Surrender the old to conquer the new. A Defender of Light understands the balance of surrendering and conquering because this is based on strategy and timing. Forgiveness magically creates a healing vibration. What is trapped can be released and what is released is free. **Freedom will always stand as the greatest of causes.**

Some beliefs demand a more direct approach to dealing with misfortune. Atonement is a method of overcoming the past and is usually attributed to paying a debt. Atonement is associated with appropriate suffering to create freedom. In the end, "all truths will be realized," and, because Forgiveness is a virtue, it is also the inevitable conclusion of Atonement. Ultimately, to forgive yourself will conclude one's Atonement and payoff the debt your universe may have manifested, unless of course you've grown comfortable with your pain. You will find, as the winter transforms into spring, that by shedding the hardships of the past a whole new life can emerge. As in a Celtic "Imram" (mystical journey), the primary conclusion of most transformational journeys end with an act of forgiveness. If there is no forgiveness in your heart then there is no forgiveness that will echo back from your universe. As a result you may be living unnecessary hardships because you, yourself, hold a grudge. "As above so below" your core system of resentment exist in the center of your universe. You cannot escape it so you must learn to send positive messages out from the center and continue to reinforce that information. The messages travel through space and time to the end of your universe, and then reflect back like an echo. Whatever message you determine (forgiveness or judgment) is what you will receive. This could be called Karmic, except that warriors are rulers of their domain and freewill determines all belief. Possibly a better term might be a Karmic Warrior. Accepting the value and responsibly of your Karma and fighting back to make a better choice for improvement will change your world. This is true despite any beliefs that you must atone. If there is no forgiveness to give then you will be unforgivable. Begin with yourself, and then think of someone who makes you angry. What is it about them that remind you of you? What is it about you that makes you angry? Now take arms against your Anger and may the day's battle win freedom for your heart. Try this affirmation, *"I can now forgive myself and others!"*

Forgiveness is the 9th of the nine challenges for the Light Warrior.

LESSON FIFTY-TWO

Turning Truth Into Reality

Nine Challenges of the Light Warrior

To become a warrior is no small task. To become a Defender of Light is no small honor. If you commit to this path, there will be many sacrifices. This adventure has many challenges, and will require more courage than of all your ancestors before you. However, to be a Defender of Light plays a magnificent role in the destiny of people. People have lost the understanding of the second word in Human **Being;** they have forgotten what it means: **Being** Human. To awaken from amnesia is difficult in the beginning, but it gets easier. Clarity requires effort and discipline. In time, your disciplines are integrated and evolves into an identity. An artist represents what he or she creates; therefore, an artist is not just a career but is also an identity. To integrate your path with an identity is necessary. It is your identity that engages your Path and overlaps into your career, family, religion, politics and community. To fully remember what a Human Being is requires an understanding of what being human looks like.

Being Human is usually referred to as a flaw in some way such as, "So I made a mistake, I'm only human". But to personify the flaw and not the ideal is missing the mark. Being human means being humane. This requires love, compassion and a warrior's courage. **A Light Warrior is both humane and a humanitarian.**

To establish your being as a Warrior of Light transcends limited self-images. A Light Warrior can shape-shift to be whatever is necessary. "This talent to 'morph' into the image required by the demands of a situation will determine how effectively you create common language". **The Light Warrior** is the warrior spirit applied to what is loving in the human spirit. This definition may seems simple because it needs to be. Misinterpretation is the bane of human error. If you take on the Light Warrior challenge, you must know that your life will change. Old ways and some old relationships will either transcend or descend. If you are willing to dedicate yourself to your Light, Love and Truth, then this is your chance to create something human and meaningful. There are nine challenges to the Light Warrior Path. Each one is as important as are fingers to a hand. The Code of the Third Millennium Warrior delivers the nine challenges to test the outdated and destructive warrior concept of yesterday. Today's issues offer a greater challenge than ever required in humanity. You, by your dedication to this manuscript, have challenged yourself. Of the millions of possible literary selections, here you are. If you believe that reading these words is mere coincidence, it is not. Open your eyes to the possibility that this is your time of power. This is your challenge and leap of faith that only a warrior is capable of engaging. Each level requires dedication, patience and power. The benefits are dedication, patience and power. Imagine yourself with this and much, much more.

Nine Challenges of the Light Warrior:

The Path of Power: Turning virtue into reality. By maintaining these nine virtues the warrior can draw upon the mystical powers of Light. The Light Warrior must fight through the darkness of night to reach the coming sun.

1st **Honesty** (Speak the Truth)
2nd **Effort** (Discipline / Maintain the Truth)
3rd **Patience** (Surrender / Accept the Truth)
4th **Courage** (Conquer / Fight for the Truth)
5th **Honor;** The Acquisition
6th **Compassion** (Love) The Experience

7th   **Respect** (Respectful of all life) Humility
8th   **Faith** (Trust)
9th   **Forgiveness** (Self and Others)
10th Sunrise (Victory and **Freedom** by Reaching the Light)
                Code of the Third Millennium Warrior

LESSON FIFTY-THREE

The Light Warrior Way

Path of Power

The undertaking of the Nine Challenges of the Light Warrior is the Path of Power. It is a virtuous quest for truth that will take you down a road of transformation and adventure. This quest is charmed with a guarantee to change your life and help clarify the mystery of lost purpose. You will encounter many people on this adventure; some will inspire you to witness a higher image of yourself and others will show you the heart of what lies in your own darkness. Pay close attention because once you begin the Path of Power all people will enlighten you to the infinite possibilities exposed by miraculous events. There is no certainty of the exact experiences you will encounter along the way. As you are unique, so will your adventure personify uniqueness. The Defender of Light is a specific image only you can see. It is exclusive to you because it has your face, and you, like the artist are the creator of your own self-portrait. The Defender of Light image can be described, but only you can see the true reflection of your purity. It must be envisioned and then recreated daily. As in the tale of the Arthurian Knights pursuing the image of the Holy Grail, so is your quest to find the image of your highest self. Unlike the Arthurian Knights, however, the Third Millennium Warrior is gifted with much more potential. Evolution dictates advanced doctrine in education, standards of living with a broader scope of human perspective. The True Earth's higher vibration has also developed the human capacity to excel and can deliver us from repressing the feminine spirit. This makes it more possible that, instead of one warrior attaining the Holy Grail, an Army of Light Warriors will rise up to defend the beauty of Light that exists in the human heart. Imagine an army of humanitarians dedicated to the pursuit of clarity, courage and compassion. Imagine the power of light embraced by an army of virtuous beings dedicated to integrity. Imagine the most negative doomsday prophecies being neutralized by the power of positive faith. If you have this seed of memory maturing within your imagination, welcome to the game and the adventure.

The Path of Power and
Nine Challenges of the Light Warrior

1st Honesty (Speak the Truth)

One must dedicate to a more honest self. Learn to speak from the heart without being cruel. If this implies cruelty, then look inward for a deeper level of self-reflection. Dedicate to the creation of your word. Become an Ambassador of Truth.

2nd Effort (Discipline and Maintain the Truth)

One must dedicate to a more passionate self. Learn to put forth the effort to question false representations without being self-righteous. By example, teach others it is permissible and rewarding to develop a more proactive lifestyle. Effort is action, and positive action brings positive results. Action is the legacy of the warrior spirit. Human beings are bred to excel, this is the birthright of all people. Without effort we would not be human. Work to improve.

3rd Patience (Surrender / Accept the Truth)

One must acknowledge the *wisdom* of letting go. Surrender is a strength and not the preconceived weakness. If there is a situation that you cannot improve, then you are being guided toward applying your efforts to accept the situation as it is.

Developing tolerance is necessary in all relationships. Dedicate yourself to a higher level of non-judgmental acceptance.

4th Courage (Conquer / Fight for the Truth)

One must dedicate to the courage of your convictions. You will face opposition that will not be kind. Old concepts may challenge your strength. Fight for what you believe is correct, even if you stand alone.

5th Honor; The Acquisition

One must dedicate to nobility with integrity. Rise above petty childishness and step forward to recognize, claim, and personify what is good in the human heart. Honor is a mystical power that breathes strength into the soul. Honor must be won. Honor is a prize that offers integrity and esteem to your life.

6th Compassion (Love) The Experience of kindness

One must acknowledge that love is the most powerful force in the human experience. Love is embraced as real magnificence, not to be feared. We are created from love and must continue to remove the layers that block our ability to relive and express it. The magic of love is what will inevitably unite us all and complete our destinies. *The power of the Light Warrior is a light that extends from the heart like a sword of Truth.*

7th Respect (Respectful of all life) Humility

One must acknowledge the grand purpose of life relates to the value learned in relationships. **Humility** is a requirement to attain the education of higher respect. Whether you are student or teacher, it is in a relationship forum that we learn and grow.

Ultimately, you will judge yourself and in the end possibly be judged by the respectful conduct that pertains to the relationships with people, Self, nature and Spirit.

8th Faith (Trust)

One must accept that all people, places and things have a purpose. Whether that purpose is perceived as good, bad or ugly, life itself is the great teacher of us all. "There are no mistakes, only tests and lessons." Trust in yourself and have faith in the creation process.

9th Forgiveness (Self and Others)

One must dedicate to releasing the imprisoned past. Unlock the chains that bind us in the finale stage of this Mystical Journey. By freeing the Fear, freeing the Anger, or freeing the Pain, you will free yourself. This is the power of forgiveness and the final challenge of a true Light Warrior.

10th Sunrise is the Dawn of the Third Millennium Warrior

After battling through the night, overcoming the darkness, and slaying your Dragons, appears the dawn of a new transformation. From here you have risen up to establish your path fully committed to a clearer destiny. *The lion heart will evolve by the power of virtue and light. The heart of the lion will shape-shift and become a Warrior of the Heart.* The Light Warrior search for other warriors of light begins.

LESSON FIFTY-FOUR

Ascending Through Light

Speaking the truth, seeing the light and walking the way: together they represent the audible, visual and kinesthetic aspects of transformational shape shifting. It is sometimes difficult to realize in the beginning that the visual (light) and the audible (truth) are one and the same vibration tuned by repetition. The voice of God (Truth) or seeing through the eyes of God (Light) is the same vibration. Understanding this idea will generate the initial alchemy. In the end, you will be able to emulate light and see truth. Practicing visual forms of meditation and prayer techniques will help comprehend the images and vibration of one's highest light. These tools aid in one's personal stability as transformational evolution is occurring. Work directly with light itself. Use breathing to take in and generate the energy. Exhale all the negatives that project shadows and block light from your soul's path. Focus is essential. A sharp and disciplined mind slices through seduction and distraction. **To change your life you must first change the concept you're in.** Training your mind is always necessary to shape-shift your vibration. It requires the desire and the drive to let go of old patterns and cynical thinking. With diligent effort you will create light and become able to embrace the New Energy. With practice you will come to see that people are more drawn to you and they may not even understand why. Practice your Art to become the Art as well as the Artist. Vibration is sympathetic; when you resonate at one level, people of like vibration are hypnotically attracted. If you sing a musical note into a guitar, the string of that note will magically respond to the tone and vibration. Vibration attracts like-vibration and all human beings are drawn to like kind. Lost souls seeking energy are also drawn to a higher vibration. Keeping a protective circle of light around you will help in dispelling **unwanted intrusion**. Visualize a glow all around you, moving and lingering from every motion or gesture. Feel the presence of energy all around you as if you're wearing a suit of glowing armor. Tai chi is an excellent way of practicing this method of moving energy meditation. Another form of protection is to visualize mirrors around you, thus reflecting back unwanted intrusion. Ultimately if you remain connected to your God source through visual aid, faith or request for higher assistance, you can progress safely at your own pace. When light charms its way into your life, you will understand how to play as children play, and yet still remain comfortable being you. You must release all anger, fear or negativity because this is the foothold darkness has on the middle world. Negativity blocks the motion of light. Just by releasing negative thinking and emotion, your energy level will vibrate higher, allowing higher spiritual messages to communicate with you more comfortably.

Turn off the room's artificial lights, turn on music for vibration, close your eyes and try feeling every movement as your light and the air merge, whirl and flow. Try to create the pictures in your mind, thus manifesting the image. At first it may only be an imaginary image, but do not abandon the practice because you are on the correct path. If you can see it you are halfway there.

In the beginning visual skills just unlock your imagination to the possibility. It's the power of the imagination combined with physical effort that has created all that people have ever built. Coupling imagination and warrior effort is the surest way human beings have to forge their existence. You will soon be able to move through a crowded room with light beaming from your body. Walking with light will develop you with powerful intent. Healing is the next phase of moment and light. Because the vibration of truth and light is in harmony with nature, light has natural healing energy. Some people don't even know they have it, and yet people are still drawn to them. Others pursue higher levels intentionally. This energy can be developed to heal both your own wounds as well as the wounds of others. Because all things are common ground within the Light, the mentally, physically, spiritually, and emotionally wounded can experience healing by ascending through light energy work. Be mindful, however, not to rely completely on others to do all your energy healing. If you choose to be a Light Warrior, you must learn to participate in the work of your journey. If you need assistance, open your world to higher levels of integration by calling upon the miracles that exist within the power of your faith. Ask for truth and light will come.

LESSON FIFTY-FIVE

Work of Art

Art can be defined as expression created through a form of labor. A painter chooses paint and colors to create magnificent works through an expression of lights and darks. An artist can create magnificent works of art, but isn't the magnificence the relationship between the art and the artist? In many ways the artist serves the art and the art gives back fulfillment. Painting with color is classically *one example* of what we think of when describing a work of art. Whether we are painting on canvas or creating on a broader canvas, we are all creating something.

Dedication and discipline are required to complete a great work. This is a rule that reaches far beyond paint and canvas. These attributes are why it is necessary that human beings have a warrior spirit. Without this drive we simply do not finish what we start. What gratification is achieved from an unfinished play, an undeveloped idea or a half written novel? What fulfillment is achieved from a lost purpose or an untrained immature warrior? So much of what we will become rests upon our preparation for the future.

Imagine yourself the artist painting a canvas. First, begin with the imagery of the painting that you would like to create. Then through an inspiration to achieve, gather together the tools and resources necessary to bring your painting to life. Find a place of comfort where you can create your art. Once you are ready, begin the next phase of creating by merging the paint, the brush, the canvas, the environment, the concept and the artist together. With the right preparation the *opportunity* for success is created. So much of the creative process is preparation. We lose sight of the value of preparation because we want immediate gratification. Many people lose their purpose in life because they do not realize their life is preparing to create the imagination of their dreams. Could artists complete their paintings if they had neglected to procure the paint? We must remember that preparation is the artist's process as well as the finished product. We must remind ourselves that what we are doing today has a value if it is preparing us for our tomorrow. Even paying our rent is a part of creating our art because we all need a place of comfort in which to work. There are so many outside forces that seem unnecessary, but from the finished product of our dreams they may be completely necessary once we look back on the process.

In the new age, creating through expression will go beyond the canvas or stage or other traditional art forms. Works of Art are how we will define ourselves. We will become a people who will recreate ourselves with passion to adjust to the oncoming world. The work we do will be to evolve, to improve and to complete our soul's journey and destiny. This is a pure form of expression and by all definition is considered the highest work of Art. **The Work of Art is you**. You are the creator, the laborer, the visionary, the poet and the passion of your life. It is you with the gift, the canvas, the paint, and the creative spirit. It is you that must elevate yourself up to the Light of God. It is you who must develop the talent and create yourself as a masterpiece. You have always had the ability to create yourself in a beautiful light. A light that will make people pause to look upon the beauty of color, the beauty of composition, and the beauty of how the light reflects. You know your lessons better than anyone and with a reawakened sense of faith you can finish the work.

In this manuscript much has been said about the lessons of our ancestors, but now you are here with the opportunity, the light, and the wisdom to lead your ancestors into victory. You can complete the final page of your personal journal in this world or not. Do not let sloth beguile your spirit once again. You are so close this time, yet sabotage is lingering over your shoulder like the Seductress that she is. Remember, one of the greatest human woes is a sin against the Arts. What happened to the poem never shared, the song written but never sung out loud, the music never heard, or the light that was never allowed to shine?

The work is you, and there is more work to be done. This is the task of a "Warrior Poet." The love that flows freely from the heart is creative freedom. Make your self with the precision of a true craftsman and the emotion of a true Artist. This work has always been possible to complete, but fear and shallow truth have denied us all of victory. You can finish the art with your unique signature. All things are possible because you have available all things that are needed. You can create yourself freely if you can allow yourself complete creativity.

LESSON FIFTY-SIX

Inner Reality

"I Am"

It is important to recognize the images of your inner-self. Your inner images are who and what you think you are. Understand these images, accept them and mold them to suit your choices, your wants, and your needs. Dreams are a part of your inner reality and are an informative medium of expression for you to decipher. Facing all your inner realities requires a strong dedication to courage and honesty. This is valor in every sense, and valor is always necessary whenever risk is required.

Facing your inner realities may not seem like a risky act; however, this can lead to a shaman's journey into the underworld where shadowed corridors and lustful Dragons exist. Also, exposing your inner world to the outside world takes the personal strength of humility. Humility is a high virtue and found only in the most disciplined warriors. Overpowering one's pride and accepting fair judgment (justice) requires the courage necessary for honesty. If your inner world is based on seduction and weakness, then it will take **courage** to face it alone or **clarity** to find the help necessary to neutralize your Dragons. Regardless of the circumstances, bringing your inner-self to the surface is an essential part of recognizing the self. Some of this reality will take shape as pure whimsical fantasy, and other parts will require extreme sober attention. Many realities may cross and overlap, such as the practical, the day-dreamer, the sexual, the obsessive, the insecure, the child, the critic, the good, the bad and of course the ugly. Nonetheless, with honesty as the vehicle, compassion as the path and freedom as the destination, victory is possible. This is all a part of learning to live a more honest, kind and free life. **Freedom must be found within.** Shedding the layers of valueless existence will help you unveil the core of who you truly are. Ask yourself if you are living your inner realities in your relationships. Are you capable of living your inner realities in all relationships? If not, then define what you're afraid of and why? Are you allowing your partner to live their inner reality? It takes real courage to face whom and what you are in a relationship. By virtue of valor the Dragon Slayer faces these fears. As a Warrior of Self, fears are neutralized, changes occur, and relationships shift. Some of the losses may be extreme; however, freedom is the opposite of oppression and living a lie is the very core of oppression. The price for freedom usually outweighs the price of pain. Sometimes through pain is the only way to **be real.**

Does your outer reality correspond with the secret thoughts that exist inside? Is your outer reality merely a projection of an image you wish people to see? Granted, if you project something long enough it will grow to manifest itself; but is the projection healthy and positive for you and your loved ones? Is your image real? Will the image you project ever be real? Is love real in your inner reality? How honest do you allow yourself to be in matters of the heart? These are all valuable questions to ask one's self. Certainly if we are conscious of our problems and are working to correct the behavior, it is not necessary to expose the process to the world. Your privacy should be determined by what is honest and comfortable, not by other people's insecurity. The focus in this lesson is more concerned with the conscious debauchery of our behavior in which we masquerade to hide our real feelings. Merge your actions together with who you think you are, what you are feeling, and the words you are the saying. Honesty is the goal.

Inside every human being are the honesty and goodness that live in the human heart. It is this goodness that reminds us that we are all human beings. By unlocking the frozen memories of our past we allow the strength and essence of our true self to surface. The individual then remembers the value, purpose, and work required to truly be a human being once again.

It is important to remember that if you believe you will fail, you stand a higher chance of failure. By the same rule, if you believe you can change the world you stand a higher chance of change. The inner and outer realities must reach a mutual and symbiotic relationship to achieve the most from your efforts. When the outside world does not measure up to your inner fantasies, you must fight to bring imagination to life. We must work today to have our dreams come true tomorrow. We must unlock the information deep within us to guide us on our true "Path." Your inner reality has a master's voice. We all have the wisdom of a Master within us to guide us to our destiny. Together the inner and outer worlds relate to create.

LESSON FIFTY-SEVEN

Defender of Light

"I Am a Defender of Light"

"I Am a Defender of Light." Within this statement breathes the power of the "Word." If you have dedicated yourself to living the lessons in this manuscript, then you have already begun to unlock generations of blocked memories. Now it is time to accept who you are. Being a Defender of Light is not easy. Changes occur and battles will be faced. There is no way around it, only through it. Reaching this stage is to rise above fear and weakness. You must dedicate to facing, and if need be slaying, your Dragons whenever they emerge. You must dedicate to teaching honestly while you continue to learn honestly. Your actions will yield a higher awareness and a higher vibration. People will be drawn to you for your strength, honesty and kindness. You will find yourself scanning the perimeter in certain situations, looking for someone to right the wrong that you are witnessing. It is in the now that you become the single person strong enough to do what must be done. This is a great burden at times and can challenge your sense of fair play.

Sometimes the ones you love will also bear that burden. It is not always a pleasurable task, but you will find that the benefits of your valor far outweigh the liability. The burden of discipline will subside as your efforts manifest results. You become the product that will be greater than you were before. You become the art. Through repetition you will simply get better at taking your rightful place among the honorable. It is then you become the Light Warrior foretold in prophecy and capable of generating great light. Unlock the image by seeing yourself as a Light Warrior and Defender of Light.

The Code of the Third Millennium Warrior is not designed to replace your religious tradition but to unlock the power of real convictions so that you can serve your beliefs on a higher scale. The Code of the Third Millennium Warrior supports and honors all systems of belief based on love, strength and kindness. A Defender of Light serves the image of a humanitarian and is dedicated to the union of all men and women.

Speak the words, **"I Am a Defender of Light."** Say them in your meditations or shout them from the highest rooftop. These words bring power and purpose. Join in the Army of Light and be dedicated to preserve what is kind in the human heart. Becoming what is kind in your heart is what creates the like vibration that attracts to you the Army of Light and vice versa. Take on this image with nobility and honor. In the coming time of prophecy, maybe you will stand alone wearing the crest of the Light Warrior. You and maybe only you will have the strength, courage and power to represent the best of humanity in a time when humanity is failing. Chaos will bring hell to the middle world and only a select few will step forward to claim themselves as Light Warriors. Others will be seduced by greed, fear, anger and so on. Riots and devastation would bring new meaning to the image of civilization. **In the end, humanity must persevere.** The Light Warriors must step forward to take on this task. It will require a warrior's strength to accept this challenge. The Code of the Third Millennium Warrior will act as a guide to prepare individuals to be ready. Living now as a good example is the key to preparedness. Once the battle lines are drawn, it could be to late. Clarity and focus develop with time and training. Those who choose Pacifism (The Art of Doing Nothing) will hesitate in the confusion, but the Defenders of Light will act with clarity because they already know who and what they are. Strong and secure in their convictions, the Third-Millennium Warrior will emerge as the champion of a new age. Defenders of Light will secure a New Dawn of Humanity.

We all have dragons to slay. The quest for enlightenment is really a very simple one. It is so simple we will look everywhere but in the mirror to find it. **Enlightenment is our Virtue** *sustaining a balance with Seduction. It is Light neutralizing the Dark to establish peace and harmony. The Light needs not to conquer the Dark, only meet it, thus exposing it. The concept is so simple, and yet the achievement is so perplexing.*

It takes real discipline to strive to make better choices everyday. It is the reality of our choices that we must live with; however, it is how we define ourselves that will generate the quality of our choices. Define yourself well and you may find your choices improve.

LESSON FIFTY-EIGHT

The Sacred Geometry of Three

The knowledge, the embrace and the integration

"Threes a charm" and this sacred number offers itself to many spiritual concepts. **The masculine, the feminine and the balance necessary to create neutrality are a representation of the Law of Three.** The Creator, the Kingdom, and the Army of Light, (*the father's masculine spirit, the mother's loving spirit and the children's learning and growing spirit*) help define succession based on the Law of Three. Energy itself is based on a positive, a negative and a neutralizing force. An atom, for example, has the positive charged protons; the negative charged electrons; and the neutrons are neutral, as the name implies. This law establishes the challenge of balance. The task is to achieve equality between the positive and the negative.

When equality is achieved balance occurs, this neutralizes the struggle for supremacy. When one force is dominant, it causes an imbalance. To regain our balance can be as easy as choosing to conquer or choosing to surrender. Achieving the power to neutralize is the highest of martial art skills. The Warrior Priest or Priestess refines this talent and offers it through example as a gift to all that are present. These are numerous examples in religion of this law of three, like the Christian Holy Trinity or the Chinese Tao (Yin, Yang and balance). We are all influenced by the challenge of this three-fold magic found in scripture. The prophet Jesus began a three-year crusade at age 30 teaching of a forgiving God other than a judgmental one. By foreboding conclusion, at 33 he died and rose in three days time to achieve ascension and Mastery. It's been said "A religion is truest when the originator is walking the planet, but sometimes in order for that religion to spread the founder must be martyred." And so the paradox of a new religion is born. This was the story, and the story will be told forever. There is even a belief that the bible and the story are still being written. Martin Luther King Jr. once said, that Christ gave him the message and Gandhi gave him the method. The inspiration of the one Christ is the inspiration of how love's power can change the world. Many will follow his example to a higher level of Light and vibration.

Christ was quoted as saying, "I am the Way, the Truth, and the Light." The Children of God will fulfill his wishes by following God's way of love, with truth (honesty), and Light (clarity through Gods eyes). Being a good example is **how** we emulate God's wishes. Christ is the heart, thus through the heart one can embrace salvation. People whose life is an example of love, truth and light without the need for judgment or prejudice are fulfilling Christ-like wishes. All people are unique and, as a result, cultures, religions and philosophies will differ. Cultures will overlap and tolerance born out of Love can be the neutralizing force between the polarities. Interestingly enough western philosophy can be defined as a quest for the truth, while eastern philosophy concerned with process, is noted for walking the path or way. Both western philosophy and eastern philosophy can be balanced and neutralized simply by Light.

LIGHT

Light is clarity.
Clarity reveals Truth.
The Truth is what is real.
What is real? "Love is real."
*What is Love? God is **Love**, God is **Truth**, and God is **Light**.*
Through Love, Truth and Light, we are all welcome in the Kingdom of Clarity.

Love is God's reality and religion is a reality defined with words. If a religion's words are loving then religion becomes a beacon of Light and inspiration. Any spiritual religion that is not based on Love is the manipulation of false prophets. If a law or knowledge feels honest to you, embrace it. If you embrace a law with passion a discipline will eventually form. With time the discipline fades to integration. From integration, the knowledge and you become one. Judaism, Christianity and Muslim have been termed as three sons of Abraham. All three are shining examples of the sacred geometry of three. **First** the law or *knowledge*, **second** the loving *embrace* and **third** the disciplined *integration*: all three in succession represent together a path described as Enlightenment.

LESSON FIFTY-NINE

The Power of Truth

"Stepping into Your Power" can be done individually or in ceremony. The combined energy of ceremony is predominately the most dramatic method and is as old as the history of people. Stepping into your power is an anticipated part of life for you as it was for the ancient members of your lineage. Accepting your path and your purpose is a profound awakening for everyone before you and around you. So few will ever experience the value of such a pure moment because facing the magnificence of who you are and who you are capable of being can unleash the Dragons of Fear. Primarily the fear of greatness and success can ascend from the forces of darkness to stifle your movement and leave you frozen in apprehension.

Human beings are the only creatures on this planet who are afraid to be what they are and even more afraid of what they could be. Human beings would deny or forget their purpose rather than accept their own gifts. No other creature on this planet faces this difficulty. Would the humming bird deny its ability to fly? Would the antelope refuse to sprint or the dolphin forget it was born to swim? So why is it that we refuse to face the power of Truth? Herein lives the mystery inside us and the mysteries that comprise our journey to find our Truth. To understand the mystery and the journey better, let's define **The Three Levels of Truth.**

1st Consciousness: The "I Am" is an aspect of truth.

The "I Am" is how we understand our sub-self, central-self, and super-self (child, self, and God). The "I Am" is all aspects of yourself, your convictions and ego. "Who am I and why am I here?" Consciousness is our inner to outer reality. It is our image of individuality, as we perceive it. Consciousness is our own personal slant on life. This is your truth or my truth as you or I see it. Your truth as you see it can easily differ from someone else's truth. The education of the relationship sends two people with different truths on a quest to find a common truth. Without the challenge of relationships we can create the reality of self-absorption.

2nd Nature: The "Natural Law" is an aspect of truth.

The "law of nature" is heaven, earth, God, Universe and all living things as a whole. This is the way of all living and dying things. It is all things, both matter and void of matter. It is what is and what should always be. As much as we try, this is beyond words and what the Chinese refer to as "Tao." This is the positive, the negative and the neutralizing forces of energy. This applies to a more harmonious relationship with the planet, God and Universe. Nature's law is not to be limited by the limitations defined in human language and yet, we must try to define it. The further we disconnect from nature the more we feel disconnected. Nature reminds us that the complexities of discovering the "I Am" are really about simplicity. Nature grounds us and yet teaches us how to fly. Nature is a great Master of us all, the gracious host to our experience.

3rd Experience: The "Process" is an aspect of truth.

To "Experience" is the "Process" of higher awareness. Theory must be tested in order to understand what is the "Truth." Experience requires a dedication to all dimensions. Experience is mostly conveyed through the realms of the physical, mental, spiritual, and the emotional. Experience is what forms the "I Am" as we interact with natural law. Human experience is what we are here to document. We are spiritual beings having a human experience.

Truth is much like a pool. It is up to you how deeply you wish to swim. The deeper you experience it the more your truth ("the I Am") and Universal truth merge closer to the One. The one universal understanding is the experience of the ancient mystery of achieving Enlightenment.

The third level of truth, "Experience" is defined as living through a process. Living through a process or cycle is what determines our continuing lessons in life. Experience promotes understanding and brings a sense of direction when no direction is otherwise apparent. Your experiences are as unique as you are. Their value may be based on pleasantries or horrible consequence. Regardless, you are not totally alone in the process and we all have work to do. Your experience is a story and has a purpose. Natural law dictates, "All things are meant to be," and it is up to you to give this truth a meaning.

Sometimes it is necessary to accept that life is as it is in order for you to get beyond the weakness of self-absorption. **Self-absorption is to dwell an illusion to Death**. The sooner you accept this, the quicker you can move through the process. The experience of hardship is the dying process in motion because natural truth is all living and dying things. You must visualize moving through it and out the other side (rebirth). Pursue the vision. This action brings faith into reality. The value and purpose of a difficult experience awaits you on the other side. In fact, a whole new reality awaits you on the other side of rebirth. You may find new relationships or other people requiring advice from your Higher Awareness. The trick is not becoming stuck. There are always ears that will benefit from your voice, and there are eyes that will benefit from the images you've seen. It is up to you to determine the methods your experiences can be best conveyed. Without experience there would be no truth for people, only concepts of undiscovered information. The undiscovered "I Am" is simply waiting for the experience to explain, "Who am I?"

Experience is why the children of life are here. Life is a grand playground of trial and error and the game never ends as long as we are alive. Seek out the value of your lessons and create something real from them. If you are uncertain what the reality of these life lessons are, then try this simple technique to turn your experiences into something real.

First, define what is real. For example, "Love is real." Love is therefore the perfect vehicle for this illustration. Second, define your experience. This is always uniquely your task, so only you can make this happen. Third, ask the question, how can I turn my experience into Love? This could possibly mean teaching or helping others with similar experiences (giving). Possibly it could be an act of self-love by caring for your own needs to promote healing. Maybe it is gaining knowledge from the lessons that experiences teach: wisdom, maturity, truth, acceptance or forgiveness. Growing is nurturing and is always an essential part of the loving process that gives experience real value. Possibly your experience may allow you the opportunity to right a wrong or bring Light to Darkness. Bringing Light to Darkness is one of the highest manifestations of a Light Warrior's passion. This constitutes an ambition to bring honesty to illusions. Helping the younger generation with advice is always a good place to start. They will need light to move forward in their processing of experiences. These are just a few suggestions; certainly once you give it some thought you would see numerous other options. It may take some creativity to decide what is the best choice for you. Regardless, there is always work to be done and it is up to you to **seek out the knowledge**. The act of transforming experience into Love is the true magic of alchemy. "Kindness magic" is the alchemy of letting love be your guide and following your heart. It is a noble challenge to be kind after battling through hell and overcoming hardships. The alchemy of changing Dark to Light is the miracle of wisdom and warrior maturity. Applying your "wisdom with kindness magic" is the manner in which real horror transforms into an act of real love. Granted, turning horror into beauty is a task for a true artist who has a passionate soul with extreme courage, strength and love. Only a Warrior of the Heart can create such a Work of Art.

"I am the Experience of Nature," is the validation of one's true power. This affirmation can lead you to a deeper understanding of where we all need to go. It requires a deep loving embrace to be active and conscious about what is natural.

Imagine for a moment that you are looking at a friend's loving face. Then step away ten feet, then step again ten times ten, then ten times ten again and again and again until you find your mind's eye seeing yourself out in space ten thousand miles away. Now imagine ten thousand times ten thousand miles more only to see your friend and billions like him/her united as one in the image of one single light. This light is moving across the heavens with a backdrop of billions of lights behind it. If you can imagine this, then you are capable of realizing that sometimes clarity requires distance. This image is the seed of our oldest memory. United in Light is the highest goal of the Third Millennium Warrior and an image for which all Light Warrior's consider to be the deepest Power of Truth.

LESSON SIXTY

Illusions

The idea of perception is the most influential force in the human experience. Perception regulates our lives from morning to the approaching morning. Perception has an almost overwhelming ability to create an illusion of control through self-identity. One's picture of one's self is the inner workings of the most complex system of perceptions congealed into a body of sophisticated concepts and synchronicities. This swirling mass of shape-shifting energy moves and creates an illusion that we as creators draw upon to form mass. The mass we form is the theater of drama that we perform on a daily basis. We all exist in an illusion of who we are. It is the drama software that convinces us what we do, think, and feel. The processing of this program manifests the image for a giant projection. Our ego is a great theater for drama and illusion. So many occurrences contribute to this matrix, such as our lessons, our experiences, our programmed thoughts and behaviors. It is hard sometimes to recognize that we have created our life as it is. It is harder to accept responsibility for our lives. This proposes an often-asked question, "Why would I have chosen this life or why wouldn't I have chosen better?" It is difficult to wake from a nightmarish dream to ask, "Why would I allow myself to go to sleep?" It is common: people want a simple answer to a difficult question. However, just as the nightmare in a dream is a part of your inner-self looking to be experienced, so are the complicated dramas we instigate on a daily basis. Too much of our reality is wasted by an immature dance we create to offset boredom. Often our lives are spent in a push-pull game based on acting out an unhealthy behavioral drama. We spend way too much time taking nonsense personally. We create grand dramas, overreact and do things we regret, only to awake in a nightmare, retracing our steps and asking, how did I get here?

Illusion is a deep and complex study. Few people delve into its **real** complexities because beyond the illusion can unfold even deeper illusions. The core of your reality is buried deep within your integrity. Your integrity will help you proceed beyond illusion because honesty is the experience of truth. It is amazing how so many Truth seekers seem to miss this seemingly simple concept. To pursue the Truth, you must become honest. If "What goes around comes around", how can one find Truth without honesty? Human beings only use a small portion of their brain, and seeking the Truth while not being honest is proof evidence of that. Dishonest Truth seekers are walking examples of limited intelligence. Attempt to see with honest eyes and more illusion will become apparent; for example, if all things happen for a reason, then why do people only use a small portion of their brain? Our ability to manifest, communicate, and tele-transport would be profoundly impacted by a more heightened and developed brain. We would be faster, clearer stronger, more powerful. So then why are we denied access to all of our brain's data? Could it be that human beings have not risen to a level of integrity to be trusted with such a power? Have you risen to a level of integrity to be trusted with such a gift? Is there anyone in your world that you believe has the integrity to remain chaste if they were given super human powers? If any of these questions have sparked a curiosity then possibly there is a direct link between evolution and integrity. If this sounds honest, then consider the idea that developing a higher level of personal honesty could lead to accessing the gifts stored in the untapped brain.

Mythology and legend are filled with challenges for prizes that only the most virtuous warrior could win. In our legends, we want someone pure hearted to hold the key and gain access to the prize or next level. This may seem like fantasy to some, but doesn't the same concept hold true for Jews, Christians or Muslims wishing to enter into the ascended kingdom? There are many dramas that we can perform to meet our wants and needs. Choose well your illusions then release them. Mold them to allow you the integrity to find access to the powers and destiny that you are entitled. Ultimately Love defines reality and filtering illusions through the heart will project images that become real. The clarity of love's light will dismiss false illusions of separation to uncover that we are one. Without this oneness the ego creates dramas for entertainment. On the one hand, our illusions of God are our own false creations. On the other hand, we are a part of the One, we are a part of God, and we are God because all is God, even our illusions.

LESSON SIXTY-ONE

The Smoky Mirror

The purpose of life is about relationships. A relationship can exist on all kinds of different levels with infinite dynamics. You have a relationship with all living things that you encounter, whether friends, strangers, self or God. Relationships are a part of choices that place you in a space and time. Some will help you and others will frustrate you while others appear to have no real merit to your situation at all. **The smoky mirror is a negative reflection of who you are or what you dislike.** It is a shadowy reflection of your lesser self without the clarity of your greater Light. Even people that frustrate you the most reflect a piece of you.

The four basic houses of our reality are mental, emotional, spiritual and physical. The four houses reflect images of each other like mirrors. Our soul reflects our thoughts, our thoughts reflect our emotions, our emotions reflect our bodies, and our bodies reflect our soul and so on, back and forth. They reflect back upon each other in an ongoing journey of education, process and purpose. We reveal ourselves through images and reflections and the reactions to these reflected images. By understanding this concept we can develop an ability to read a deeper reality just by reading what's being reflected and reading our process within those reflections. For example, the mental creative process forms a negative idea such as "I am not good enough." The emotional creative process mirrors this and creates insecurity. This reflection is fear based and is in opposition from your spiritual God source, Love. The fear then blocks our light source and creates a shadow. From blocked Light an amnesia appears to support unworthy beliefs in a separation from God. The physical reality becomes a reflection of an individual who is negative and insecure, believing in an illusion that denies themselves of their God source and self-love. Relationships with others, like relationships with ourselves, also reflect. Therefore relationships will step forward to support unworthy illusions. Feeling inadequate is created by a shadowy source and its reflections. Over time this forms a program of negative reality. If this type of negative idea/ emotion/ spirit/ physicality is not exposed, then whenever you reach a point of being good enough, a sabotage system blocks the light to support your Smoky Mirror. *The Smoky Mirror is a methodology of understanding one's shadowed self.* By studying your shadow we can become better equipped to counteract its negative repercussions. A teacher can use a smoky mirror technique to show a student a reflection of what the student is projecting. It requires the teacher to role-play the student's behavior so that the student can see his/her self. This technique is tricky and can trigger a person into an extreme reaction to his/her own shadow-self. So often we meet people in our lives that frustrate us and cause us grief. The Culture of the Forgotten Truth has taught us to judge and dismiss people whom we dislike; however these people have a purpose. What frustrates us most is the ugliness in someone that we would consider ugly in ourselves. Seeing someone who has a flaw that you have overcome in your self is difficult and annoying. After all, if you can overcome your issues then why can't they overcome theirs, right? Smoky reflections are designed to read and react to. You can also send a reflection of love and clarity to someone's darker reflections. Judgment is difficult to overcome when people present you with good reasons to judge. It takes effort.

Sign reading is an intricate part for a Truth Seeker's quest. Recognizing the most dysfunctional person can send a smoky reflection to read in the beginning. Smoky reflections have a value to your reality and offer insights to knowledge. They teach us who we are and whom we do not wish to be. All reflections have a source image and it is important to find out if you are projecting or if you are reflecting. Are you the teacher or are you the student? Beyond this analogy is the challenge to define what are you projecting or reflecting: is it positive, or negative, is it warrior or victim? Ultimately the most difficult relationships show us either the best or worst of ourselves. The beauty is that by bringing forth the darkness you can expose it to Light. The people that brought you pain, sorrow, and grief also taught you how to find ways to overcome pain, sorrow and grief. Put that value to good use. No matter how difficult or how insignificant, all relationships in life have their purpose because the purpose of life is about relationships.

LESSON SIXTY-TWO

Messengers of Light

We are all created in the image of God, descendants of Light and heir to an inheritance. There is a fortune in treasure that we have not even begun to claim. We are people created in the image of Light with birthrights and enormous God given potential. The Messengers of Light who have accepted their path have had many names throughout time, and we have grown accustomed to hearing their stories. From scripture or prophecy or religion or science, the Defenders of Light make their way to the forefront of recognition and even martyr their lives for our benefit. It is necessary for us to have these examples of Light. However, we need not detach ourselves from these people by choosing only to witness their grandeur. Living a good example is the purest calling of God's children. Living a good way by example is an act of virtue. A virtuous example will in the end attain the highest respect. As you know, speaking words and living your words can be two different things. Some believe that it's necessary to spread the word of God to prove one's worth; however, this act can sometimes be construed as intrusive or offensive. How can it be that the best of intentions are sometimes met with such negative responses? The relationship with God is all encompassing and uniquely personal. Instead of always voicing the Word of God, try hearing God in every word. It is far better to be invited into one's spiritual ideology than to project your views onto someone even with the best intentions. Some people are led to believe that spreading the word of love is the same as living a life of love. It is not. Talking and living are only equal if they coexist in a pure heart. Do you possess a pure heart? If you pause to answer, perhaps it would be a greater strategy to approach a higher level of one's own relationship with God before judging others. Your actions will be closely scrutinized if you too are a work in progress. Living an example of honesty serves us better. Revealing a solution to salvation is a powerful calling, and one must understand it is filled with great sacrifice. Christ tried to teach people to live by his example. Scripture proclaims, by following Christ's Way (compassion), Truth-and-Light that heaven would open. Many people have interpreted this to separate themselves into an us or them split. This type of thinking works only on the surface of truth. We must learn to dive further into the pool of deep truth. The key message is to follow his example or "way."

The Chinese refer to life's natural path as the Way or "Tao." The Christ-like way is following a path of love and living an example of a pure heart. This declaration is so powerful, so profound, so crystal pure, that for thousands of years even the slightest redirection can miss the mark and lead to unnecessary hostility and bloodshed. **The Way of Love is simply living a life based on compassion doing the work of forgiveness.** Spreading the word (Love) works beautifully when you live compassionately throughout your life, which in itself will inspire others. A lifetime of love will never go unrecognized. All God's children are welcome into the Kingdom of Light. It only requires a life based on **clarity, honesty** and **compassion** (Light, Truth and Love). Whether or not you tell a good story carries little merit in the Kingdom of God. Only the life you have chosen to live will give you the salvation you deserve. There is no manipulation that will overturn the final truth of Justice. A Light Warrior recognizes the Sword of Light rises up from the pool of deep truth that exists in the heart. If this light emerges from your heart it is yours to claim. If clearly you've been blessed as God's messenger with the gift of teaching the Way, then know the weight of the sword you carry. Live what you teach. This is no small undertaking, and as a Defender of Light, **the darkness will mark you as an enemy**. Stay strong because being chosen to be a Peacemaker is a high honor for the Light Warrior. Light Warriors will fight to preserve freedom, but to be able to share a freedom that is indescribable is truly a God-gift. If you have this gift, then go forward and teach your gift to the world, but remember you are here to learn. Learn from your teachers, learn to be a teacher and then learn from teaching, for this is the **Circle of Light.** The circle of light is the path of the enlightened. Is your soul still on the path? Fewer than one in a million souls still forge their way on the enlightened path. If you are here to become and teach the Truth with compassion, then in you lives a miracle within the message.

LESSON SIXTY-THREE A.

Teacher

"Show Me The Way"

Only those with shallow foresight will argue against a dialogue of peace. This lack of vision is why the Light Warriors have to become the teachers of the new dawn. The importance of teaching, especially through example, is unparalleled in the evolution of people. Even in the most common of situations, teaching is considered a grand and noble calling. Never should a tutorial exchange be dismissed as trite. It is a challenge for your potential to move yourself and others forward. Many people are afraid of this opportunity, feeling that they are unworthy of such a task. The most common excuses are, "I must learn more before I can teach," or "What I do cannot be taught," or, "I don't have the time." This is the rational way of dismissing who you are and the work that needs to be done.

Unquestionably, teaching an experience does require effort with an understood scope of information. Whether it is physics or honesty, teachers must define the information clearly in their minds and then convey it using the power of the Word or the power of example. Clarifying the lesson within the mind's eye is how a teacher learns from teaching. Humility, for example, is a grand lesson for a teacher to give, but is much better delivered by example than by punitive action. Thus, being humble can teach humility. However, as in all cases of education, it is up to the teacher to determine the best manner by which to convey the instruction. A good teacher doesn't try to teach from a higher place commanding information down to a student. A good teacher transforms to the level of the student to seek out a language that can be heard. Being heard is the most important challenge for a teacher. Speaking a good message has little value if it cannot be heard. A good teacher searches for the language and as a result the student teaches the teacher how to become a better teacher. There are three things to remember if you wish to become a good teacher: The greatest **Tool** is listening, the greatest **Challenge** is to *not* play the Master Guru and the greatest **Technique** is by example.

If you have been asked to teach, then you are being asked by the universe for the information you have to offer. If you do not feel ready, then by acknowledging that you are still a work in progress, begin your first lesson with a lesson of honesty. You will always help your student by being an example, which is more educational than you may know. By accepting your inadequacies as a teacher you can become more efficient as a teacher. This is the self-realization that develops once you accept the role as a teacher. Understanding your weaknesses is one of the rewards that your student will give back to you on this road of educational exchange. If you have ever been called upon to enrich the value of someone's life then you understand the powerful exchange that occurs when you teach. **To be labeled a teacher is one of the most giving and time-honored professions known.** Without education, humanity would be aimlessly lost. A teacher is the one profession that transcends all social classes. It is possible that the most desecrated soul can teach the most prominent and brilliant scientist something of value. Society cannot break down the powerful exchange of evolution that is mankind's destiny to learn. People need to learn because they grow discontent in their stagnation. Even if the information is simply asking for directions, the importance of that information determines a student's immediate destiny. This smallest classroom parodies the universal classroom of life experience. The desire to develop is growing as the remembering and the gateway sheds light on who we really are. As the human race evolves, the need for instructors becomes increasingly necessary. For millennia we have considered ourselves separate from each other. However, now with gateways and communications opening around the world, we can realize that we have always been working together. This is the process of information being transmitted to the masses by way of the teacher-student exchange. One person teaches another to use a hammer; the student then erects a wall that becomes a home that becomes a neighborhood that becomes a community, that becomes a city and so on the process continues. Whether we accept it or not, we have always been working together. We are all connected; we must continue to help each other along. To deny your brother or sister the help of your experience is to deny the value of your own destined humanity. A real teacher is based on who you are, not just what you know.

LESSON SIXTY-THREE B.

Spirit Training

Light Warrior Training Method to Shape Shifting

0) **Memory of Light** (Awaken, Moment of Truth, Clarity)
1) **Expose the Shadow** or dragon or weakness (fear, seduction or addiction)
2) **Explore the Potential** (compare present situation to "What would I be like if . . .")
3) **Work the Body** A body must be able to metabolize the transition (Honor the Temple)
4) **Discuss the Character Flaw** (behavior patterns of weakness)
5) **Seek Out the Correct Question** "Who, What, Where, When or How?"
6) **Analyze the Question** (remove all blame from the equation)
7) **Begin the Internal Journey** (plant the seed that positive change is now)
8) **Define the Fear** (what is blocking or slowing you down)
9) **Face the Fear** (leap of faith and courage)
10) **Propose a Real Solution** (Victory) What is Victory?
11) **Visualize the Solution** (vision, clarity, light) Turn toward the Light.
12) **Diagram the Program** (strategy and planning)
13) **Discipline the Program** (gracefully apply daily)
14) **Release Old Negative Habits** (Surrender)
15) **Replace with New Positive Habits** (Conquer)
16) **Document Progression** (reaffirm memory) create a teacher outline from experience
17) **Explore even Higher Potential** (surpass comfort zones)
18) **Set Higher Goals** (student becomes a teacher)

19) **Allow Fear, Seduction or Weakness to Gracefully Dissolve** (Neutralize)
20) **Celebrate the Victory and Peace** (There's a time for work and a time for play.)
21) **Light Exposes more Shadow** (The journey begins again from a higher place.)

LESSON SIXTY-FOUR

Weight of the Sword

"Knowledge is power." Power is energy and energy can be measured. A Light Warrior carries the power of responsibility as if it were a friend and close companion. The Light Warrior sets an example of virtue. The Light Warrior holds an example for others to aspire to. The weight of the Sword is responsibility. The level in which you take on this weight is valuable knowledge to anyone who chooses the power of a warrior's path. The warrior-artist understands the correct feel of the sword handle, the length of the blade, the polish of the steel, and the distinct individuality of the temper line. The magnificence of all the elements—wind, fire, earth, water and steel—bring you in touch with mind, body, heart and soul.

It's a good feeling to hold the right weapon. It's a feeling that has power and grace that magnifies when allied with honor and destination. A virtuous purpose allows you to cut through the air as if you owned it and together your spirit, flesh, and metal merge as one. This is you elevating above the simple issues while using your divine gift of creativity to unify you with the purpose of heaven on earth. As above in spirit, so below in your stance; you must create balance.

It is a grand feeling of empowerment to acknowledge that your past battles in life have prepared you for whatever awaits lurking in the shadows. With sword in hand connected with passion, you can easily perceive that you are now ready. However, you must first clearly understand the real weight of the sword. *The Light Warrior has a sword of truth extending from the heart.* Taking on a warrior's path you must learn the value and consequence of every cut. The purity of your actions when armed may not always be in plain judgment of others, so you must always be in plain judgment of yourself. This judgment must remain honest and void of denial. **Denial is a charm and talisman of Darkness.** The sword has always been a symbol of clarity; however many have lost their vision while under its powerful influence. You must know where your power lies, and if it can better a situation or destroy it. Few things cut as deeply as a lack of accountability. Not taking responsibility is a recklessness that dishonors your value and brings shame to the line of nobility that has fought bravely to bring us Truth. Search your soul for accountability in every situation. The correct choice depends on it. If you cannot accept the responsibility of your actions, then put your weapons down. This too is responsible because it shows you are wise enough to know that more tactical skills need to be learned before facing your greater Dragons.

Fighting is a birthright, but sometimes one must learn to fight the need to conquer in order to succeed. Wisdom is wholly critical and is the essential element needed when weighing the responsibility of the sword. You must recognize that when a warrior moves into action, the actions are designed to be effective. The repercussions of that action can, however, weigh heavier than you wish. If you choose to lift a weapon for needless battle or selfish seduction, then the thing you want most will devour you. Wants and needs are not always the same thing. It is a mature warrior who has learned to want only what he or she needs. To be a Defender of Light you must choose to lift the sword only for Truth. As a result, we take on the weight of honesty and our challenges become our disciplines. Many people believe themselves to be a good person, but few people have the discipline and character necessary to really be good people. As a Defender of Light, you must learn discipline and learn to look honestly at yourself. To be a good person requires commitment to that image. Contradiction only delays the process and adds to the number of your lessons while old age and lost time creep closer. The purer your path the faster the cut, and, in some cases, heavy is the weight of the blade. For some this means conquering to win, and for others this means fighting to let go **(Surrendering to Victory)**. The Third Millennium Warrior does not quit and cannot be defeated. To be able to call upon this power on a natural level is inspirational and a grand example. The Third Millennium Warrior must attain balance or all life on this planet will suffer for generations to come. **If the warriors of the future cannot find balance the world will be destroyed.** Are you still waiting for easier signs to read? Indecision can get you lost, as can a Dark path contrary to nature. The inability to act with strategy is wasting the God-gift of free-will. Make an honest choice and blame no one. A Light Warrior's blade is always double-edged and polished to reflect the true self.

LESSON SIXTY-FIVE

The Culture of the Forgotten Truth

How does one begin to convince someone that their views of reality is an illusion based on a victimized cultural protocol? To insult your reality or way of thinking is undoubtedly a delicate matter not to be taken lightly. Even with the best of intentions, when questioning someone's belief system, it is easy to create unnecessary conflict. Together we must put forth effort to find a language that can be understood.

The Code of the Third Millennium Warrior speaks into what has been and can now be remembered. It is the voice of the awaiting Truth broken down to study. This manuscript reminds us of the courage that already exists in our hearts. Feel it, hear it, and acknowledge it as a catalyst for you to remember who you were meant to be. You and you alone have the sensitivity to understand what's real as it is dispersed into your life. The Truth can be a lightning bolt of brightness that may flash only momentarily for a glimpse of recognition. Time presents the perfect gifts. The gift is in the first instant of composed clarity, unencumbered by forces such as ego or arrogance. It is in the first intuitive reaction, and for centuries it has been simply called "A moment of Truth." Understand that a moment in time is as long as the initial intuitive reaction. The second-guess lives in the second moment. The second guess is the premise of uncertainty devised by the Culture of the Forgotten Truth. It is with second-guessing, that your intuitive perceptions are set aside.

Granted, many decisions in life are complex and deserve deeper research. However, your initial thought should be placed in a position of high prestige. Thus, you develop a practice of comparing all options with the initial moment of intuition. This helps create a safeguarded determination. It is the intention of the Culture of the Forgotten Truth to persuade you **not** to listen to your intuition, but rather hear a sales pitch that only clouds your intuitive instincts. The sales pitch convinces you that other mundane directions are better choices over your original thought. This is how human beings forgot who they are. People have lost their natural instincts to react with intuitive action. Ancient civilizations were not as encumbered by such salesmanship. Granted, we consider ourselves more evolved than uncivilized people, yet we have forgotten the intelligence of nature. Fight or flight is the term used to describe some of our basic instincts. To conquer or surrender is the basic choice. To neutralize requires balance and is the third choice.

The **Culture of Forgotten Truth** is a program of lower integrity. It is the lost or forgotten ideals that must now be reinstated. The Culture of the Forgotten Truth is a life based on stress or fear. It is a life based on seduction or addiction. It is a mainstream of reality that inhabits and oppresses. Propaganda and misdirection can be anyone and everyone that accepts or decrees a false or superficial existence. Life should be rich and fulfilling. Anyone who chooses mainstream protocol **over** instincts and divine purpose has put destiny on hold. Anyone in your world that would deny your destiny because they have denied their own is who personifies your obstacles. This is a battle of logistics. The depth of a false world versus the depth of a real world creates this challenge.

Imagine on one side a mass of media propaganda skillfully devised to sell the masses on a concept. This concept is then perpetuated and implemented into everyone's life till it becomes everyone's normality. Now we have mainstream cultural normality brought face-to-face with you and one single gut instinct that believes something is not right. It's you against what everybody else is doing. Now remember the Culture of the Forgotten Truth was designed to control you with fear, but this is not a battle to control, it is a battle of trust and faith. It becomes your moment of Truth delivered on a lightening bolt. It would be so simple to ignore it, because moments do come and go except, it happens repeatedly. Your destiny is personal but not passive. Denial is a magical charm of darkness and millions fall helplessly to its power. Soon, the doctor destined to heal disease chooses instead to become wealthy, or the teacher destined to combat ignorance chooses only to observe, the artist forgets to paint and the parent neglects to come home. The examples are as infinite as the excuses we make on a daily basis. How easily do you sacrifice yourself for no better reason than, it's expected? If sacrifice sounds too familiar, its time to open the eyes of the sleeping lion within you. Only courage will claim what is truly yours.

LESSON SIXTY-SIX

Honoring the Temple

The heart is an instrument for our love and it is with this belief that the heart is the altar of God. Within this treasured chest we receive the communion of our kindness, mercy, compassion and forgiveness. It is with the heart that God is experienced. It is here where the highest remembrance of the human being is stored. A pure heart is sacred. The heart is the Truth, Light and the Way and only through a pure heart will you enter into the kingdom of heaven. The Sacred Heart is Christ-like. The messenger's physical form has little merit to the value of a message. The heart need not be described by race, religion, color, society, or gender. The heart is the coming sun for a new dawn. There will be a time when the Warriors of the Heart will step forward to claim what is sacred about them. When this awakening occurs, all of heaven and earth will shine for these people. It will be a time of a great gathering and celebration for any who choose to honor God's altar. Heart filled enlightenment is the purest memory of the human being. Try not to become rigid to what your eyes see or your ears hear. There is more to being human than sight and sound. It is the heart that must transmute the message of humanity into a life based on compassion. Many will preach that "The bible says . . ."; however, the bible speaks no words out loud, it reads a message of personal internal truth. The bible's message is a personal understanding acknowledged between you and your highest master. It was designed to aid you on your personal spiritual journey. If one interpretation does not carry the message of compassion, then seek further for the deeper meaning. The Truth is there, but it is up to you to find the way. The Code of the Third Millennium Warrior is designed only to aid you in taking part in choosing your own clarity from God's messages.

Question all interpretations that seem curious to you. This is not to say, "Throw the baby out with the bath water." Do not dismiss ancient teachings; instead dig deeper for its original knowledge and determine if you have been led accurately. Profound Truth exists in our ancient teachings. Unfortunately the Culture of the Forgotten Truth will spin a translation to best support limited ideology.

There are even people that believe Love is an omnipotent force, but are scared to fall in love. It's up to you to uncover the real Truth behind the secret walls of illusion. There is still much to be rediscovered from our ancient text, because so much has been forgotten. Even Christ questioned the interpretations of scriptures from his day and time. He spoke against old interpretations and offered new insights. If you follow his revolutionary example, clearly Christ's message was not always found on paper, but in the heart. Most people would rather not take part in their own development. So like sheep they accept shallow information and are content. Others would throw their hands up into the air and say, "What's the point, its all propaganda, why even bother?" Denying possibility is just as weak as blindly following misinterpretation. You will not change a situation for the better if you run from it. Both strategies are weak and show a blatant desire to avoid challenging oneself. Misinterpretation is the bane of human existence. Bigotry cannot support the message of love and therefore becomes contradictory if presented in a spiritual religion. When bigotry is spoken the heart is silenced and the doors entering the Temple of God become closed to the outside world. Unfortunately poor spiritual leadership can allow this to happen under the pretense formed by the best of intentions. This lesson is not aimed at doubting scripture but it is directed to challenge spiritual leaders to do their jobs better. Where is the justice when spiritual leaders believe they must lead only certain types of people to unconditional love? It is in these situations that the tolerance found in the heart, the Temple of God, is needed. The heart is a messenger, a filter, an image, and a reflection. It is a sanctuary and a vessel for transport. It is where your virtues feel safe. The heart gives strength to the weak and wealth to the poor. It offers a source of morality and identity. The heart can create joy and can give joy to others. The heart is the greatest alchemist's tool of our species. It has the potential to change the worst into the very best. Herein lives the Temple of God and it is in this chamber where the Light Warrior must find solitude to achieve victory and fulfill his or her own personal destiny. The heart is the savior of us all.

LESSON SIXTY-SEVEN

The Kingdom of Clarity

Seeing through God's eyes

All warriors with a virtuous heart will be honored in the Kingdom of Light. The Kingdom of Light commends all achievements by the Defenders of Light and rejoices upon their return from a noble journey. Great celebrations wait for the warriors who conclude a journey because this moves us all to the next step in spiritual evolution. You might say that you chose not to be a warrior and believe that you will also be welcomed into the Kingdom of Light. All who choose a virtuous path will indeed be welcomed; however, it takes effort to maintain virtue. The concept of a warrior is applied effort to a purpose, taking personal responsibility. This means overcoming blame and judgment. Placing blame only deflects responsibility and creates the illusion that you had no power.

Blame and victimization are twin sons of the same mother. Warriors always have power. The Dark Warrior is destructive; the Light Warrior is not. The evolved warrior or Warriors of the Heart apply their efforts to the highest good. To deny the concept of a warrior is to deny your defenses against facing your fear. Without the warrior spirit, fear will block you, seduction will distract you and addiction will weaken you. The Culture of the Forgotten Truth would have you deny the warrior, which would lead a sheep to the slaughter if it served a false illusion of cultural protocol. Your culture breeds pacifists and even convinces you that pacifism has some sort of nobility. This is a lie that betrays us all. It is naive to believe that you were embodied in this life to do nothing. **Pacifism is the Art of Doing Nothing.** Nonviolence in the face of violence is not pacifism; it is fighting with a peaceful strategy. To face violence with nonviolence requires the courage and strength of ten warriors. Pacifism is a seduction of our warrior birthright. You are supposed to be here and you are here with a purpose. Empowering yourself to find and serve that purpose requires effort. Effort is the march down the warrior's pathway to victory. There are many examples of great Defenders of Light such as Mahatma Ghandi, Martin Luther King Jr., Moses, Buddha, Christ and others. They chose a nonviolent path to achieve higher victories, but to say that they were passive is absurd. The Third Millennium Warrior is inspired with these examples in mind. These Defenders of Light personify the core strength necessary to engage the Darkness of Ignorance and dethrone it with Light. The will and sheer determination necessary to change cultural protocol from Dark to Light requires tremendous strength and it is an inspiration to us all.

The Light Warrior bears close resemblance to the legendary Arthurian Grail Knight Percival and Galahad. Legend has it that Percival was a warrior with both an iron will and the capacity of the Christ-like heart. He was a Warrior of the Heart and capable of finding the Holy Grail. The legend says Galahad was simply born with a pure heart that made him worthy to find the Grail and the Truth. Both examples underscore this: **it doesn't matter how you find the Light just as long as you pursue it.** In legends passed there are only a few warriors evolved enough to be a Warrior of the Heart; however, now an Army of Light Warriors will engage a new age with new energy. Percival placed the image of the Holy Grail in front of him and chased it to death's door. He gave his word that he would not quit and he honored his word. He persevered to victory.

Place the image of your highest ideal in front of you and chase it. Take who it is you wish to be, project it, create around it and then become it. Use the Strategy of Focus and see with your greatest capacity to imagine and remember. Imagine a cord ascending to heaven from the top of your head. Practice seeing the connection with your God force and allow that energy to accompany you wherever you may venture.

The Creator is with and without time, with and without energy, with and without space, with and without matter, the father the mother, and yes, both Light and Dark. The creator is above the battle of Light and Dark. We unfortunately are not. The creator guides us to balance and creates harmony. The creator is beyond the myths and images that we have given God. God is unique and unifies all things. God's purpose is unity. The idea that "Man was created in the image of God" has always been the highest self-compliment man gives himself to proclaim his existence. Creating unity and balance perpetuates Mankind's highest good. Man has always flattered himself with the concept that God's image is us. We hold tightly to this idea to give value to our kind so we can reign supreme over the other creatures on this planet. Unfortunately, there are real questions that arise to a human parent-like image as the Father and God: Is God a super-conscious or possibly the most perfect image of ourselves that we can achieve with our imagination? Ultimately we are left with our own pursuit and our own unique interpretation. We must all find our unique Truth. We must all find our own way home to God. It was initially important for some cultures to **not** name this force that we worship to redirect our human needs to individualize God as a being. Possibly God's real name is unpronounceable or simply beyond words. Over time, the God with no name still took on a human-like identity known as the Father. This makes sense because the Father, of course, is a creator of children in his image.

For some reason it is still necessary to place a physical form on our creator no matter how many times we clearly exclaim, "God is Love." The Holy Trinity describes God in a three-fold way, exemplifying that a single word is insufficient. Love is God the Father, the miracle of love is the Holy Spirit and the sacred heart is the Son and is God. The Holy Trinity beautifully illustrates that the single most powerful action/ reaction is to live an example of Love. This poses the question, if God is love and we are created in the image of God, then when we are not loving, how did we block out God? What are your personal images of love? Overlapping a physical idea with a spiritual idea can sometimes offer different interpretations. Our human images can make the spiritual experience very confusing.

Consider this image. There is an image of light that surrounds every person. Beyond that there is an image of light that surrounds all living things. This illuminated body of light is referred to as an aura which science calls an electromagnetic energy field. It is the energy vibration of life and creation. Light-vibration-energy is the creator's image that we were created in. Pure light has no concern with gender, race, sexual preference, social class or even religion. This is why the Light Warrior is unencumbered by prejudice. Separation is the opposite of God's unity and therefore exposes bigotry as the religion of Darkness. It is the Light that is common to us all and all-living things. We are children of Light and as so, are maturing along with our understanding of divine Light. In time, our Light will grow and evolve. The distance we have journeyed to our higher self is personal and matters little in comparison or competition with other people on their personal journey. We all have a different dance with a different interpretation and yet, we all share common ground. We all have the potential to reach our higher self. We are all a part of the One, and the One is a part of us. Just as we are a part of our physical parents, so are we a part of our spiritual life giver. We will ultimately return to the Light and the journey will reach fruition. Thus, all the great Truths will be remembered and the puzzle complete. This is the highest accomplishment for anyone and is the greatest challenge mankind has ever faced. The richness is so vast that it has taken millennia's just to remember the journey itself. In the past, the journey's end remained elusive. Only a chosen few were sent to help us along the way. Now, however, we can augment the process. The Gateway has opened and we are just an imagination away from reaching our free-flying potential. It's in front of you and it lives behind your eyes. It's filled with

Love, Truth and Respect. You have touched on it and you have toyed with ideas about it, but you may have never realized the true potential of your imagination and vision. Projection is a grand concept of inner and outer theater. You are on the stage and in the front row. In your theater are the dreams of fulfilled promises and the salvation from hellish nightmares. Christ believed we could create a heaven here on earth, a place found naturally through prayer or deep meditation that will lead you to love and peace. It's the image that Percival saw in his mind at the beginning of his quest and felt in his heart when his quest was over. It's the place where your soul's journey will be free. It is here that virtuous hearts will find victory, clarity and peace. This is the image of a magnificent Kingdom of Clarity and beautiful Kingdom of Light. We are all welcome in the Kingdom of Clarity, and it is here that we will see what God sees.

LESSON SIXTY-EIGHT

Occult

In this progressive age, many more are experiencing the seer's gift. Our young are exploring psychic phenomena that transcend the guidelines of the preconceived scientific education. The evolved children of the third millennium *(Star Children)* are growing with new vibration and expanded cerebral function. The Star Children will be the generation that pioneers the stars. They will take our legacy to the outer limits of this solar system. To pass along humanity to these Star travelers is one reason the Light Warriors were awakened.

Human beings have evoked a level of semi super-consciousness with the ability to create their imaginations. Imagine needing a tool and you encounter someone with the very tool you need. Imagine thinking of someone, only to have him or her call the next day. This happens all the time. Our day-to-day reality manifests to explore the depths of our imaginative creative ability. The gateway has opened and an expanded consciousness is here. This is not magic and yet, it seems magically coincidental. There is power in other dimensions and many are feeling it without any real understanding. Without teachers in humanity the integrity of our children will reach temptations beyond our experience. A new dawn of excitement could lead these gifted children to seduction and disaster. If the heart is not open the new energy can get stuck and become volatile, dangerous and destructive. *Without discipline and virtue the warriors of the future are destined to destroy.*

The spirit world is not so different from our physical world. It is a mirror image of what we know as our physical world. Psychic oracles read this mirrored reflection to see back into our lives. **To all those who are intrigued by the mystical**

realm be warned! This is not a vast new playground where you can maneuver as you please without repercussion for your actions. You may believe it's a carefree frontier open to simply indulge your desires as you see fit. If this is your belief then you have been deceived and seduced. There is no such world of unaccountability in creation. Creation is a balance of night and day. "For every action there is an equal and opposite reaction." It is divine reaction that reestablishes balance. Use the Code of the Third Millennium Warrior as a guide to understanding Light and Dark. There are rules and laws in every realm within the universe. Always remember the prime rule, which if broken, will open a door into the Black Arts: **"Never impose your will upon another for your own selfish gain."** This rule defines Black Magic. Cross this line in the spirit world and you enter into Black Magic. The rule is straight and narrow and without question. This is not a game! To justify your impure seductions is a waste of time. If the damage is done, so be it. Move toward your virtue and prepare yourself for repercussions and combat. All God's gifts have a seductive Dark-side and the gift of supernatural ability is no different. Just like the gift of partnership can turn your physical and emotional world dark by the act of betrayal, so the Black Arts can turn the beauty of your spirituality into something vile. Open the Dark door and you open the gates of hell to flood your spiritual world. This drama may seem intriguing to some, but it is simply a fool's journey. Until you have come face to face with pure evil, you know nothing of its devastation. If you play with Darkness you will pay a price. You must have faith and listen to your inner wisdom guiding you to make better choices. Clairvoyance, telepathy, telekinesis and so on, require discipline to develop. Oracle arts are ancient gifts that serve best for the pure at heart. If you think a question at the same time a card or stone is turned which has a meaning or answer, then the question and the answer came together for a reason. The law that all things happen for a reason is the oracle's power. The fallacy arises from the human equation. Human beings are imperfect and so are human interpretations. Misinterpretation of ancient knowledge is the bane of human existence. Oceans of blood have been spilled through poisonous misinterpretation of God's word. Language can be slippery; therefore remain honest and disciplined. Use angelic protection when venturing into worlds you know nothing about. Lost souls and sometimes Dark ones will be attracted to you. They may try to attach and can block your energy. Seek out teachers that are pure and disciplined. In time, the seer's gift can evolve. Use common sense when choosing healthy or unhealthy practices, "The mystical arts carry no weight on the battlefield." *(THE ART OF WAR)*

In battle, sorcery is no match for the Light Warrior.

LESSON SIXTY-NINE

Honoring the Feminine Spirit

Nature
"The Last Holy Crusade"

The feminine spirit is the spirit of nature. For thousands of years we have been separating ourselves further from nature and her spirit. Deep within our soul is the memory of natural human relationships without separation. Separation is due to an act of self-manipulation that has unbalanced our place in nature. This imbalance is stemming from mankind's need to control. The health of nature itself has suffered from our misdirection. Pain and fear are born out of the hunger to control. Control is a desire created to give men and women something to do. It is a desire to be dominant.

Domination wastes what is pure and clean in nature. The feminine spirit is all around us. The feminine exists internally and externally in nature for every human being. Human beings are creations born from the feminine. Man is a part of woman and woman is a part of man. We are one people with one planet. Yet, men and women are continuously reminded by cultural and social bigotry that we are vastly different. These differences are primarily life experiences based on programmed protocol designed to make men, women and nature relate through contradiction. Men and women are intended to be allies that are allied with nature. Yet the separation continues. When men and women dismiss their adversarial programming to adopt a philosophy of respect, amazing things occur. Respect reminds us all of our place in nature. In nature the feminine spirit must be respected to internally and externally achieve balance. **The feminine spirit must be honored in order for the madness of separation to end.** Nature must be allowed to flourish as it was meant to. Children must be taught to respect the feminine spirit. New doctrine must be proclaimed to enhance our appreciation so that all brothers and sisters respect the mother of us all. Women too must open their eyes to honor nature and the beauty within themselves. Both male and female must remember the value and beauty of the feminine spirit and dedicate themselves to the service of that elegance. When the feminine spirit is forgotten or abused a price will be paid. Take the time to honor the feminine aspects of yourself. Take note that we all possess these qualities and they are necessary for a healthy life. Donate service to the nurturing side of yourself and to nature as a whole. Even samurai warriors were required to write poetry to balance the masculine warrior archetype. Nature is the one true teacher of us all. Take yourself back to nature to understand this spirit in yourself. The feminine archetype breeds life. The supreme masculine archetype breeds' death, and the two work hand in hand to create nature's never-ending cycle of birth, death and rebirth. The two are inseparable. No one is completely masculine or feminine. Paradoxically they seem separated, but they unconsciously work together as allies in the ongoing mission of creation. Until now a programmed separation would split the feminine from the masculine.

In the dawn of a new age comes a new vibration. Undetected a great planetary shadow will grow to cover the earth mother like an Ocean of Evil. The sons and daughters of the earth mother will be forced to mature and care for their hurting matriarch. **The soul of the human body and the soul of the earth body will merge to become one and the same.** *A holy crusade will spring up from this alliance. A light will shine from the heart unto the great planetary shadow as if a great sword of truth emerged from the hearts of all Light Warriors. These Warriors of Light will step forward to represent the Light of humanity. By honoring the feminine and dedicating to the service of the True Earth the last holy crusade is born. The spiritual leaders of the world will gather circles of Light. These* circles will unite religions, races, colors, creeds and genders to form a giant circle of Light. The circles will continue to expand until they cover the planet. This will neutralize the Ocean of Evil. The shadow once exposed will subside into the void from which it came. This is the vision and prophecy of the **Tao of the Dragon Slayer.**

This Prophecy was envisioned with this summary. However, note the vision was witnessed with far more devastation than described in this lesson with multiple possibilities. It will all be determined by those who have faith in their virtue versus those that pursue their seductions. **A holy crusade must remain virtuous.**

LESSON SEVENTY

The Epithet of Shame

Water, Fire, Air and Earth are the elements that breed life and carry death. It is the power of the great elements that determines our existence on this planet and will ultimately conclude our existence if we continue to show them disrespect. The tribes of our forefathers have all warned us of our recklessness, and the burden of our actions, which will bring hell to the lives of our children and our children's children. We can no longer accept blind lavish impulses to fuel our self-indulgence. From now to the conclusion of our journey, all of us must assume responsibility and dedication to our salvation. The dedication to the elements will determine the destiny of mankind. This is the challenge, which will decide the refuge of the human race. If we do not achieve salvation, no excuse will be sufficient in the judgment of our kind. The Fires of hell will ascend to murder and destroy all that we care about. The Water, with its waves, floods and poisons will drown out our hopes. The Air will bring toxic winds to kill and devastate. We will no longer be nourished by the land but will be purged from it like vile creatures that are waste upon the great mother Earth. The childishness of our actions will become so apparent that the profanity of man will be the only legacy left for generations to come. God will weep at this destruction knowing full well it was our choice and the doings of our creation. The creatures of the woods and sea will despise the very scent of man and will wish that we be wiped off the planet. The spirit world will flood its demons into the middle world as the remaining people will abandon their hearts and join in with the evils of Darkness to destroy everything left that is chaste and pure. Hell will reign supreme in the middle world, as bands of evil will move through the world circling and crushing their victims while raping the remaining children of their virtue. This is a horrific prophecy for the dawn of man. In the rise of our finest hour, humankind will lose purpose and shall deliver us willingly to the Ocean of Evil that would damn us all to Darkness. Look closely at the children playing because they are the product of mankind's greatest hope and will collide with the slaughter of man's future. We will accept that decay, disease, rape and murder will become the norm. The world will grow Dark and the Light will fade in the hearts of people. An anti-Christ-like movement will grow. Chaos will dictate the future as mankind continues to control what has already failed. Man will have learned nothing as propaganda is dispensed to control a broken spirit. The controlling of chaos with chaos will become a New World Order. Man will slip deeper into his own despair. Evil and Darkness will ooze from the hearts of both men and women, and virtue will be laughed at as if it were a child's game. Horror will become the game of choice. The deeper the levels of evil the higher the prize will be given it in the name of strength and of the "Doing of what must be done." Much blood and sorrow will represent reality. **This is man's Epithet of Shame and the Path of Sorrow.**

However, it does not have to be this way: Spawned by the winds of change and rising up from the mist comes a sacred gathering. As the fog clears humanity is at the verge of a great awakening. All around us circles of spiritual leaders are coming together to embrace the challenges of ignorance. We have lived many lifetimes in this lifetime and we are unlike any generation before us. The human race has been catapulted into an awakening. A unique force new to this world rises to step forward. This unique force is you. The Light Warriors will unite in order to neutralize man's greatest despair that is the Epithet of Shame, the end of humanity. This prophecy will awaken circles of Light to emerge and they will represent the essence of courage and compassion left over from previous generations. The Ancient knowledge of choosing virtue over seduction will dictate the direction, and the Defenders of Light can and must set the example for us all. Our remaining virtue will be the driving force for salvation and will bring humanity to its feet with honor. These new warriors (both men and women) will carry hope, truth, and above all strength to their most virtuous convictions. The Light will grow and neutralize the darker vision. The shadow will fade as sunrise on a new world brings Light.

Here you have the three faces of prophecy: The negative, the positive and the neutralizing. The outcome is clandestine, because so much is still up to whether you have the foresight to move beyond selfishness. Hold tight to your humanity. It is the memory of our greatest hope and the source of our salvation. Humanitarians, referred here as Light Warriors, will offer the way home.

LESSON SEVENTY-ONE

Army of Darkness

In every life the power of Dark consciousness spews forth negativity onto one's path. With poisonous intentions for the weak at heart, evil hordes move steadily unto man. In every century this has begun small, then spewed into a massive sewage of discontent. This evil has come forward and chosen leaders throughout time, and it will do so again. It first creates a mirage of salvation, and then with despicable deceit, it will masquerade all malice and persecutions until horrible acts against humanity occur. The names of some of these leaders were Adolph Hitler, Gengis Kahn, Napoleon Bonaparte, Pol Pot, Joseph Stalin, Mao Tse Tung served their Masters of Darkness and have been justifiably condemned for their crimes against humanity.

Beyond the famous, what of all the others that have fought anonymously and then faded back into their Darkness for refuge? We all face the challenge of choosing our identity and intention. History can define and even predict a massive spread of evil, but our history denies the core levels of hatred necessary to rise up and find such people. Like fingers that reach out from hell, evil touches those that will not accept purity. Virtue lingers beyond their ability of discipline, and hate born from seduction is the only Master they serve. It's difficult to believe that these powerful men knew the outcome of their fate. They most assuredly made one Dark choice after another, allowing the power of seduction to embody and consume them. In most cases you may not even be aware that you are allowing your seductions to lead you into some other direction. The power to block Light is the power to create a shadowy illusion. Awareness is the key, but a key will not unlock a door by itself. What is more important is the effort.

Not feeding one's Darkness takes discipline. How is it possible to overcome an enemy that feeds off your anger? How do you not feel resentment for those whose actions lack integrity? How do you not choose judgment when it is certain your position is righteous? It is sometimes difficult to recognize our negativity during a seemingly appropriate reaction. Your present moment may carry many negative motivations when your Light is too blocked to see clearly. If so, you are not alone. You must see yourself for what you truly are and see yourself for whom you truly are. Do you defy hate groups with hatred? The philosophy of a false Prophet is "In a world of lies, an untruth is fair play." The philosophy of a true Prophet is integrity. However, ministers of Darkness (false prophets) will come before us with their seductions and illusions. These false prophets will elude the masses with debauchery, anger and temptation. People forget their hearts when seduced and addicted. To overcome adversity the Light Warrior will be necessary to establish peace through neutralization skills. Because adversity is not always the work of Darkness a strong heart, a strong mind, and a strong body will always aid you with the oncoming changes for sustain-ability. For everyone committed to the path of Light there will be numerous people totally seduced by the path of Darkness. Those unable to choose will be caught in the middle and have little relevance in the great challenges ahead. Many souls will become aimlessly lost and vulnerable. The lines have been drawn and strategies are in play. The friction manifested from the face-off becomes the struggle, but by balancing the opposing forces with your Light, a stalemate can create peace. Do not fear the Darkness because you can be protected by Light, but first you must **honestly** represent Light to claim your power and protection.

Free will allows you to be creator or destroyer over your life. It's the one gift that confirms we are created in the image of creation. It's given to you in the hopes that you will use it to find your humanity. However, finding your humanity is not a requirement of free will. Choose battles carefully. "Know your enemy." Know them inside and outside of you.

Evil is among us and an Army of Light must be gathered to be prepared. The Darkest doomsday consciousness can be neutralized by the consciousness of Light found in the heart of humanity. The fingers of hell will soon reach up to find new leaders of Evil, and as a Defender of Light you too will be marked as an enemy by Dark intentions. Stay strong and do not feed the fear or hate. You must learn to fight without fear, without malice, and without anger. You must learn how to fight without any negativity at all. This is how an army of Darkness can be neutralized. Light Warriors together can achieve peace.

LESSON SEVENTY-TWO

The Battle for Freedom

The Art of War

The art of war is based on the strategy of competitive engagement. Both war and the warrior can be perceived in many ways. Most nonviolent people would oppose war, yet a war against violence is a battle fought for peace. Fighting a battle for social change is a war. Fighting for what you believe in can be defined as a war. War is a word that most people equate with destruction; however, the Light Warrior wages a war against destruction, against ignorance, against wrongful violence and against bigotry. The Light Warrior's truth is that the heart of the warrior must evolve into a Warrior of the Heart. This may seem like a contradiction, but it is not. The Light Warrior spirit is confidence over cowardice. It is courage over fear. It is love over hate. Understandably most preconceived warrior images are the fighting, warlord figure that knows only battle and bloodshed. If this is your image, you are not alone. The warrior of yesterday leans much toward an outdated concept of man and his struggles to reign supreme. The Dominating Conqueror unable to surrender has found many difficulties in today's more civil culture. This new and enlightened age offers healthier images of the warrior archetype such as the woman warrior, the eco warrior, the civil justice warrior and the compassionate warrior. This new age of warrior evolution is the product of the Light Warrior awakening and a battle foretold from ancient tribal tradition.

Strategy

Moving with direct intention to a targeted goal requires the strategy of **linear** focus. "The shortest distance between two points is a straight line." You may encounter obstacles but as long as versatility and a clear image of your goals are secure then you can persevere. Moving in a **circular** path can gain momentum and strike from an alternate direction. Paradoxically both circular and direct paths require flexibility. Flexibility is important both physically and mentally if you wish to move with grace. Weapon to target (bull's eye) is a combination of recognizing opportunity, adequate preparation, and the warrior's will to make it happen. A backward movement slows the process once you commit to a technique or strategy. If you pull backwards to gain strength before moving forward you can become vulnerable to an attack and counterproductive in attacking. Unless drawing an opponent in, **strike from the position where you stand at the instant of an opening.** Empty your mind. Move with natural instincts. Too many concepts lead to hesitation.

Indulging in past tragedies is dwelling in illusion, which leads to Death. Be present and proceed now in the moment. Learn to strike with swift bursts of effectiveness. Too much thought signals that your technique is coming. When it is time to strike, implement your technique and move swiftly to target without hesitation.

Creating strategy requires knowing yourself and assessing your opponent before a technique's execution. Analyze your strengths and limitations as well as your opponent's. This insures the cleanest cut. It is important to breathe as well as maintaining a healthy life force through war and peace. Conflict is not foreign to life but a part of life. All aspects of life can be perfected. Most people become paralyzed in the initial moments of battle unsure of when to attack or when to wait. There are few conclusive rules in war, but one is clear, **"Invasion is a declaration of war."** *The Art of War* by: *Sun Tzu*

This is a law of war that should be reflected upon in individual conflict as well as in escalated confrontation. If your perimeter has been invaded, accept this as a declaration of war and time to focus your strategy. Note that war can be waged in many different ways. The Code of the Third Millennium Warrior does not advocate wrongful violence. The highest victory of war is "No bloodshed with an acceptable peace." **Nonviolence is always the highest and purest victory!** However, if invaded and war declared, the destiny of victory or defeat has been engaged. Victory is a God-gift to every human being capable of mastering the elements to his or her necessities. Be creative. If there is an achievement that you have wanted, draw in all the components at your fingertips to make it happen. All too often we miss the devices or talents waiting to be utilized in the next room. In the end, most often it's the strategic warriors that are survivors.

Just Be

"Be like water"	flowing, surrendering and conforming
"Be like wind"	move as an independent force, free and unattainable
"Be like earth"	strong, steadfast and constant
"Be like fire"	overwhelming, conquering and consuming
"Be like the void"	move through non-linear time as if you were the master of time and the master of your own destiny

The above five are from the Book of Five Rings. A great warrior wrote it over 350 years ago. It is based on five elements and strategy. The warrior believed that victory was all around us. He believed victory was God's gift to Mankind. It was simply up to the Master strategist to find it. To him it did not matter if there were one opponent (obstacle) or twenty, because victory was waiting for the one who could best use all the elements that were available. The warrior's name was Miyamoto Musashi. Legend has it that Musashi was the greatest master-less samurai (Ronin) that ever lived. He did not believe in defeat. His life offers an example of a talented, disciplined warrior with a controlled state of mind. Discipline and focus can overcome negative thinking and negative emotions. Discipline develops clarity and power. Overcoming fear is a warrior's necessity. Fear will block your progress, handicapping your pursuit of victory. If fear is apparent your freedom has been invaded, and **"Invasion is a declaration of war."** The Battle for Freedom begins when fear compromises your perimeter. The challenge must be met to neutralize the Darkness and bring clarity and peace to external and internal conflicts. To be a truly good human being requires kindness, generosity, compassion and a service to the dedication of integrity. Virtue has an essence, and a warrior's discipline is necessary to maintain it. A Warrior of the Heart is about being a good, powerful human being, and actually having the discipline to live well. A humanitarian is a Warrior of the Heart, because this is an example of strength with a life in the pursuit of passion. A war for peace and the Warrior of the Heart may seem paradoxical, but only because it is a new way for a new day. If you have focus and compassion, **together we can fight for the right to nonviolence, together as Light Warriors we will fight until we are free.**

LESSON SEVENTY-THREE

The New World

In the beginning, there was Light and a whole New World was born. As humankind is created in the image of creation, likewise in the beginning of mankind there was Light and a New World was born. Man's origin was created to discover, challenge and test the boundaries of freedom. People will continue striving to understand their value, as freedom will be redefined and more clearly approached through harmony with the true Earth. In the third millennium, mankind will create with a thought and bring forth a New World of rebirth. The coming new age will bring new philosophy, new religion and new purpose. All this is a result of the New Energy. Not all will be able to assimilate the New Energy. This is simply because of choices made to remain fixed to old patterns. It is difficult sometimes not to discern over those who follow a different direction, but a choice must be honored. It is ancient wisdom to accept and honor the choice of another, especially those closest to us.

Due to steady and more recognizable shifts in consciousness, DNA, and vibration, the battles of the Third Millennium will expedite images of propaganda and fashionable perception. DNA will develop to higher levels as our abilities and talents develop with it. Manifestations from faith become increasingly available. The human race will modify one by one and the body will endure many sometimes-difficult changes. The possibility to live longer and neutralize disease will become a more natural condition. Healers will unburden sufferers with a touch. Thinkers will explain beyond the realms of human physicality. Religions will be simplified and unified. The gateway has opened and chosen people have already begun this evolution. The dawn of a New World is upon us. Even experiences of horror will be transformed through the heart into forgiveness. Like straw spun into gold, the heart possesses the power of alchemy. DNA strands are evolving and we are remembering what a real human being remarkably is. People will move objects with a thought. People are shape shifting and will shift form from one dimension to another. We are finally choosing to accept the birthrights that God has bestowed upon us. Unfortunately before this occurs many old paradigms have to be shifted. This will cause fear, panic and violence. As people grow to change reality with a thought, fear will be the primary thought for people afraid of change.

The Battle of the Third Millennium will be a Battle of Consciousness. It will be a mass of people's positive thinking against a mass of people's negative thinking. The clash will be noticed mostly when old, outdated beliefs meet a new world concept. The New World is a concept of a merging global thinking. Global thinking is the power of concept thinking motivated by a unified presence and armed with the courage to overcome fear.

The battle of Light and Dark consciousness will not be neutralized until fear and evil are met. The showdown is taking place internally as well as globally. It will be the conclusion of the selfish, old-world order based on separation and segregation. It will be the rise to a great and magnificent breed. Light Warriors will step forward to claim their birthrights and their honor. Light will emerge, extending out from the heart in men, women and children. A beacon of light, generating from the chest with grand and noble intention will point the direction to Truth. Changes will be difficult for some and losses will be great. The laws of nature dictate, "The strong will survive." Strength, however, will be determined by information coupled with the passion in one's heart and not by brute strength. Clarity, Courage and Compassion must be combined to form the strength of the Third Millennium Warrior and a New World to come. Stand strong and you may live to see it. Stay close to your humanity and complete your soul's journey. You could be that beacon of light that attracts wandering souls to salvation. This is a true purpose and a real destiny. Do not let life slip away as if you have no control. **God has ordained you with full control.** "It is for us the living, dedicated to the great faith, not to let those who came before us die in vain". Every man, woman and child has a great task which precedes a great responsibility, which also insures the survival of our own greatness. This greatness is the power that shines through the human heart. It is in the heart that you will find the image of you as a true master and it is here that the New World begins. This is a great power, and with it, the power of Light can protect you. The power of Darkness will protect its own. The Code of the Third Millennium Warrior neither denies nor disrespects the power of Darkness. Evil has grown strong and it is a worthy antagonist.

It is true, "Sometimes the Dragon will have its day." That is why preparedness and dedication are essential. Evil will claim those who have lost their way, and emptiness will find those who are undecided. It will be then that the Light Warriors shall be called upon as an army of Light and guide the drifting multitudes into a New World. Defenders of Light will possess the strength to take the human race into a New Age. The strength of the pure hearted will be needed to represent and to preserve the greatness of all people. You too could easily be a good man or a good woman. These simple descriptions have real honor and will withstand the test of time. Honor is a Universal truth and must not be forgotten. The imprint that is being left by you is beyond your wildest comprehension. You have no idea how important completing your destiny is to us all. If judgment and prejudice can be replaced with compassion and forgiveness, then even the dogma of established Laws of Thinking can embrace a common religion of peace. Imagine the spiritual leaders of our time uniting in a nonviolent crusade to end violent war. Imagine an army of Light uniting to save and serve our planet. *"Imagine all the people living life in peace"* (John Lennon).

What if the human race were to reach a level of semi-super consciousness and could create their darkest doomsday prophecies simply by uniting their thinking power of hate and fear? The doomsday manifestation is mankind's Epitaph of Shame and yes, it is now possible. This is why we are the children of prophecy, but luckily the gateways have opened and this is a call to **dis**arm. This is a request to counter balance the judgment, fear and hate-based consciousness with tolerance and determination. The earth too will transform as a result of our changing evolution. The earth spirit and earth body will align with the human spirit and the human body. A much more symbiotic relationship will occur. People shall adopt a respectful relationship with the world. Together with a common thought, and a common purpose our good intentions are essential to create a New World.

LESSON SEVENTY-FOUR

The Awaiting Universe

Beyond the Illusion of Self Absorption

There is more to remember than you can imagine when you first embark on destiny's quest. Unlocking memory is like diving into a pool of experience, going deeper and becoming freer than you were before. Setting free old issues that hinder your development is a surrender to victory. By exerting effort into the strategy of surrender, blockages are removed and you are allowed to step forward into the next chamber of the awaiting universe. Many people are afraid of the next chamber because they fear the unknown. The past seems far safer than the future. However, the future is where your destiny awaits. The Awaiting Universe wants you to succeed. Knowledge is power, and power is the prize of a real education. As you move closer to your higher self, you will acknowledge the benefits of Listening to the Dimension of Thought, thereby easing into the Art of Doing. Liberation awaits when we **listen, learn, and do.** The healing process has many layers, as does the Master's path to the true self. The information uncovered may amaze even you. As you shape-shift into new images, old habits will lose their ability to influence you. All human beings have an ability to shape-shift and therefore can overcome fears, seductions and addictions. Recurring patterns work in cycles and should be broken in order to move you into a larger cycle of the Awaiting Universe. As the universe expands so do we. If these patterns are not broken, a never-ending cycle will continue. Transformational healing or alchemy unfolds the mysteries of these cycles by removing blockages (layers). **Addiction is a weakness that occurs when the Warrior Spirit is lost or forgotten.** Most addictions have little to do with the substances that are craved. One must dive deeper into the pool of truth to the source need that has been replaced by substance. It requires discipline to meet the inevitable challenges that await you when your fears, seductions or addictions decide to swing back around. Victory upon victory will transform the old patterns brought on by weakness and will elevate your world into the next level of the Awaiting Universe. The size of your universe may seem a mystery, but the answer is simple: **a warrior determines the size of his or her domain.** It is your will and imagination that expands your universe. Imagination is the seed planted by an early intelligence and is the driving force of the human desire to expand. The human spirit naturally expands with the universe, except that we with our imperfections can hinder this process. The human body is continuously healing itself twenty-four hours a day. It is self-absorbed illusions that hinder the healing process.

It takes a lot of perseverance to let go and move forward. Pay attention to the messages coming your way. Information is being revealed all around you. You are not alone because we are all involved. Body and spirit are merging into a united oneness. We are all merging with the earth and spirit. One statement heard over and over will finally unlock your imagination to evolve. Listen to repetition. Some will read this manuscript and dismiss it as old news. Old news is a fitting description for Ancient Truth. It is the statement, *"I've heard all that before,"* that has corrupted the soul by expanding one's ego instead of one's universe. If you continually hear the same information over and over again, then you have been targeted by that information. This means that you are either supposed to learn from it or teach it. Truth that continues to surface is confirmation and to dismiss confirmation is ignorance. If you are further along in your truth than others, then this manuscript is designed to convince you that you should be teaching. Denial of your responsibility affects us all. It is up to you to expand the conscious universe, and there is always more work to be done. Surround yourself with other creative people and create

Circles of Light. Prepare and unite people for the circle. Gather who and what is necessary to create the work. It is said, in prophecy that the gathering of the Light Warriors will grow to sixty thousand and beyond. The gatherings have begun. Apply your courage to letting go of old paradigms and segregated beliefs. Discover more about yourself by discovering more about others. Focus on what is common, not different. Prepare yourself and others. This can be done if a doctrine of respect is the common law that is enforced. Combine the warrior spirit (effort) with spirituality (grace), and then unite other Light Warriors. This is the mission of the Light Warrior in the expanding universe. Begin now. The universe will not wait on you forever.

LESSON SEVENTY-FIVE

Ocean of Evil

Even in this age of transformation and rebirth, darkness looms over us with a deep malice. We would all like to believe that evil is a solitary devil with horns and a tail; however, evil is a spiritual term used to expose an unkind spirit. The devil image is created by evil itself to preoccupy our thoughts as we allowed harsh judgments to grow. The ego's self-importance has let us toy with the idea that a face-off with a single devil-like individual is a battle we can win. This individual representation of pure evil is a ploy that allows Darkness to bide its time and grow stronger. This use of negative illusion as a tactic is a strategy of evasion. This strategy has been handed down by Darkness for centuries and has proven itself to be lethal. The truth is that you have welcomed self-destruction into your life, time and time again. The very thing that tripped up your ancestors, has also come for you. History repeats itself, and as the ancient masters have predicted, this tactic of passing Darkness through ancestral lineage has proven itself worthy. However, with the increasing ability people have to create with a thought, now an Ocean of Evil arms itself.

It will take nothing less than an Army of Light to neutralize the doomsday thinking. Now is the time that all great warriors must ready their thoughts. Choose your disciplines well; it is up to you as a Defender of Light to unite us all. Unity is our greatest hope, but harsh judgment masks the bigotry that feeds the Ocean of Evil. Do not wait for death to beat down your door. Unified Light can expose deception, but unfortunately this evil has grown strong through greed and self-importance. Seductions are creatures that we must learn to individually master. In addition you have met with hardships that have blocked your life. It is when we become warriors and overcome hardship that the unpleasant experience sustains our personal growth. It takes the discipline of courage to overcome one's fear, and seductions represent a test against Darkness. However, that was nothing like the Ocean of Evil that is waiting. The great enemy is the source evil that would manifest a global challenge. Darkness is among us and the battle is here. Remember your humanity. It is this collective union of knowledge, defended by warriors, that is our greatest endowment. As you go forward as a beacon of Light, others will choose Darkness. Darkness is a part of our world and that is why it is so familiar. One warrior alone is no match for an Ocean of Evil. Only the ancient magic of Love, Truth and Light can expose the Ocean of Evil. This warning is not designed to frighten, but to empower you into readiness. Do not focus your attention on one evil man, woman or devil. Evil is malice created by consciousness and spread with a sales pitch. The Third Millennium Warrior will believe in compassion, honor and courage to see through illusion. Because these warriors represent constructive effort and not destruction, they will empower mankind's evolution into a new dawn. Defenders of Light live as an example of humanitarians and inspire others by this example to do the same. Darkness is void of Light and it takes the warrior spirit merged with Light for the Light Warrior to do battle with spiritual evil.

Christian prophecy tells of a beast with seven heads. It is written that it will emerge in a time of dissension to create chaos. For centuries people have mis-defined the Beast. The Beast is simply a manifestation of Darkness based on Christianity's seven sins. The Beast with seven heads (much like the Dragons in this manuscript) is a metaphor for the sins or seductions of mankind. The anti Christ is a metaphor for a movement that is in opposition of the Christ-like virtues, for example, anti-love, anti-truth, or anti-Light. The seven deadly sins in Judeo-Christian text are Pride, Envy, Anger, Gluttony, Sloth, Greed, and Lust. These sins represent what seduces one over and into Darkness. The seven heads of the beast define the "WHAT," but the true mystery has always been "HOW and WHO." This brings us to the eighth of the nine seductions of man. The **Strategy of FEAR** is a primary tactic of seduction because it opposes love. The ninth seduction is the great **Illusion of DECEIT**. Deception is the mask behind which the Breast conspires. This is an illusion of Light when only Darkness beats in its heart. Perpetuating fear and cloaked by deception, the Breast with seven seductions is man's own manifestation. Seduction is the one embarrassment that we welcome with open arms. Listen closely for the sales pitch designed to deceive with an illusion that manifests fear.

LESSON SEVENTY-SIX

Light Warrior Circles

Part I

A higher chain of command filtering information down to a lower level delegation works well in times of chaos and dissension. However, an Army of Light is based on equality. The pyramid structure of a sovereignty system is based on control with a single leader and followers. On the other hand, a circle structure is based on unity with a continuous flow of energy. A Light Warrior Circle is a circle of leaders.

Congregating a circle of leaders is designed to generate a continuous flow of powerful energy. When dealing with leaders the ego can be a powerful force that must be handled carefully. It is necessary to have a kind-heart balanced with youth and wisdom for this to be successful. A higher level of clarity and peacemaking is imperative to create this forum. Clarity, strength and compassion are required to unite a powerful circle. The balance of conquering and surrendering is a necessary strategy to attain your goals. To develop an Army of Light Warriors, one must gather together a circle of people inspired by humanity and willing to merge. The warrior circle is a proven and ancient practice. It is not an easy task to begin a warrior circle; however, the power, which comes out of the first one will inspire everyone to new heights. From then on the circle will begin to empower itself and participation becomes increasingly pleasurable. This lesson is a guide to help create your own warrior circle. It is just a guide. It is not a mandate.

1st. Candidates must be studied for their value and their ability to participate. Meditate on this before you begin sharing your messages physically or telepathically.

Once certain, initiate your desire to participate in the Army of Light by speaking of it and seeking out more information. People will take notice, some will be drawn to you and some will not. You must have faith that the people who are supposed to unite will step forward. Listen closely to all messages because once the Light Warrior commitment is made a power ignites. With this commitment both the forces of Light and of Dark will take notice.

The conditions for a warrior candidate are simple. They are as follows:

A. Each prospective member must have chosen their path, be able to define that path, and that path must be dedicated to **Light**, i.e.; *Way of the Artist, Teacher, Giver, Visionary, Path-finder, Peace-keeper,* etc. As long as the path is dedicated to bringing about clarity, it can be self-explanatory or uniquely creative. It does not need to be overly romanced, i.e., a lawyer (Justice), or a Doctor (Healer) or a businessman (Trade) etc.

B. Each prospective member must be a **Warrior**, meaning they have given up all claims of victim energy and take full responsibility for their own actions. These are leaders and controllers of their own destiny. Often but not always, these leaders will have an established group or circle that they are in charge. Sometimes they will be at the beginning of a teacher or leadership role and the Light Warrior Circle becomes a catalyst.

C. Each prospective member must be guided from a power measured by the love and compassion in their **Heart**. The prospect should be considered an example of what is good in the human heart. A humanitarian or someone who wishes to be more humanely conscious is your best clue.

    A.   Light

    B.   Warrior

    C.   Of The Heart

Light Warrior of the Heart is the Third Millennium Warrior.
The Light Warrior Circle is a multi-philosophical, multi-denominational, multi-cultural, co-gender event. The Light Warrior Circle *is not* designed to be a healing circle. Instead, it is a warrior's challenge for leaders to converse, unite and step over into a higher level of power. It is the intention of the Light Warrior Circle that after the ceremony each empowered leader will return to their lives and use their gifts to teach and to create their own circles for sharing and healing.

2nd. Each candidate must be prepared by taking the time to create a trusting relationship. In that time a path is determined for or by the candidate that is based on their personal life story.

3rd. A date, place and time are established for a preliminary gathering.

4th. An invitation is sent to each candidate to request their participation in representing their path in a circle of warriors. Lesson seventy-seven (The Gathering) is an example of an invitation. It is written in the style of this manuscript; therefore you may wish to reconstruct the invitation to your personal liking.

5th. If all the candidates have not met, it is good to bring them together in a social gathering first. Introduce everyone together and explain in detail what this is about and what will be required. Once all the points are covered, step back and allow the circle to form. Remember, this is a circle of warriors and taking the lead of leaders is a delicate matter that must be allowed to happen, not forced. Together plan a date for an all-night ceremony.

6th. Plan an agenda filled with three elements.

A. Time allowed for each member to step forward into the circle by announcing their path and sharing it with the other members. It is necessary for the candidates to consolidate their life story into a tight version. Because of time constraints, about 15 to 30 minutes is fine. This requires introspection from the candidate and is helpful in personal realizations.

B. In the time allotted, each member should be encouraged to share his or her personal path in the form of a ritual or gift-giving experience. This can be a tea ceremony, a peace-pipe ritual, a gift, a lesson, a poem or anything that is the sharing of an experience. This portion is designed to create unity.

C. A warrior's challenge is necessary to develop strength. Nine sessions of chanting meditations or prayer works well to challenge and to expand consciousness. Tantric yoga, Kundalini yoga, the Rosary, spiritual singing songs, martial arts, Buddhist chants and Native American spirit drumming rituals are just a few methods to help bring the spirit of your creativity to light. It is recommended to use several spiritual paths and cultural languages to create an even a higher sense of global unity. This releases the shadows of bigotry from the circle. Depending upon the number of participants and level of difficulty, nine challenges of 11 to 31 minute sessions is more than sufficient for one evening. In the beginning you may wish to start at the 11 minute mark and perhaps build upon that in Gatherings to come. **Be creative.**

7th. On the night of the Gathering ask that everyone come early so they can carefully review the agenda, and bring food for the morning sunrise. Also, having everyone help prepare the site together helps a united purpose.

8th. Prior to the beginning of the ceremony create a protective grid around the perimeter of the ceremony. There are a few ways different cultures go about this task such as; placing crystals at the north, east, south, and west boundaries along with activating them with tones, burning sage, tossing sea salt, saying prayers, calling in the Holy Spirit in all four directions, etc. Once a vortex of protective light is established the ceremony is ready to begin.

9th. Begin the ceremony by allowing a brief prayer from each member of the circle to bring in the spiritual Light of each path. Everyone must be honored with complete respect for his or her participation. Start with a light warm up to loosen the spine, then proceed with the agenda. Do not dominate the proceedings. You should allow it creative flow, yet be sure to find a way and keep fairly close to schedule so as not to carry the ceremony late into the next day.

10th. **Sunrise** represents victory by reaching the Light. Celebrate victory with food.

LESSON SEVENTY-SIX

Light Warrior Circles

Part II

(The Purpose)

*"The Light Warriors will be called upon in a time of
Darkness to step forward and represent what is best
in humanity."*

Herein lives the alpha and the omega of The Light Warrior purpose. **It is a call to disarm.** In these words real purpose can be remembered. Light Warrior Circles will be gathered in times of Darkness chaos, war, famine, pestilence, and destruction. Wherever there is Darkness the Warriors of Light will be summoned and assembled. It is here that the power of strength and compassion be united in a spiritual communion of sacred Light. The Warriors of the Heart will take their space and let their presence shine. Circles of Light will emerge from the prayers, chanting and the power of Light that comes from the Heart. The Light Warriors will form a circle *to neutralize* Darkness, thus creating peace. These Circles can go any and everywhere. The circles will unite and the circle of Light will expand to sanctify entire surroundings. The formation of Light will grow stronger as the prayers and vibrations unify with the spirit of the True Earth. It will then expand across the land and water to blanket the furthest reaches of imagination with the illumination of Light. Exposing Darkness with Light is the Light Warrior challenge, purpose and mission. Those who choose this will be required to fight wrongful violence with nonviolence. Violence itself may represent the image of a Dragon to slay. **Nonviolence is the intent of a true Holy**

Crusade. Focus *not* on the faces of those who do dark things, but instead focus on neutralizing their desire or intent. Inhumane intention is the real enemy. The highest victory is an acceptable peace. Those who take this on will be required to live a great example. Those who take this on will face many sacrifices and many rewards. It will not be easy, yet this is the opportunity that will put you head-on with your greatest self. Once again, it would appear your time to fight has come.

LESSON SEVENTY-SEVEN

The Gathering

A Circle of Light

Invitation

In every life the power of negative forces intersects and influences one's path. Everyone faces the challenge of choosing a positive or negative identity and intention. All those who choose a higher path must establish dedication and courage. However, in this changing age, the image of a lone seeker on a journey is not enough. A new and faster age is making it necessary to unite these seekers of Light to create new possibilities. One person is no match for the Ocean of Evil that is manifesting from today's negativity. Yet, it takes only one person to accept their God given birthright to Light. It takes the desire of only one person to accept their power and purpose by merging the warrior spirit with the clarity Light brings. One person can step forward as a leader and create a Circle of Light. By creating a roundtable forum where no one sits at the head, we can empower the individual quest for Light in a gathering of Light Warriors. A unified table designed to share and enlighten with individual experiences of each warrior's life intention creates the Light Warrior's "Circle of Light." By sharing in the power and knowledge of each warrior, we can unify powerful experiences as a whole. Unified as Defenders of Light we set an intention upon the planet. Committed intention challenges all warriors to claim their birthright and accept their responsibility of leadership. The Light Warrior Circle is not a healing circle, nor is it a circle dedicated to any one religious tradition. It is a circle of circles. It is a circle of united leaders that can reach out to unite intentions with other leaders. As leaders of Light we can share even higher levels of spiritual work thus, develop and grow. From one gathering, other gatherings can emerge and more warriors can take their rightful place as teachers of humanity in this changing age. Beyond that, even a greater number can manifest and in time an entire Army of Light will stand. All warriors will stand unique and united led by the passion and virtue from the heart. United together is the beginning of the greatest army ever constructed to represent hearts filled with strength, love and compassion. Imagine one individual heart beating in harmony with a mass army fueled by Love and Light. Imagine a positive consciousness that will grow and neutralize the negative doomsday consciousness. A nonviolent army unencumbered by race, religion, color, creed or gender would have infinite creative possibilities. We could create hospitals for the sick, shelters for the battered, along with education for the less informed. You can step forward to overtake the Darkness of ignorance and fight to preserve the greatness in the human heart. Your imagination is not limited by anyone but you. The time has come for you to reach out with the power you have developed and touch the hearts of other leaders of Light. Together we can create peace.

The Challenge

_____,

You have been recognized and chosen as a warrior and Defender of Light. It is with much enthusiasm that the Light Warrior Circle is requesting your participation in an all-night warrior ceremony. This event is designed to awaken an ancient spirit for a new breed of warrior. The Third Millennium Warrior is a warrior of the heart. The Light Warrior is a humanitarian who has developed his or her life to the dedication of a greater-self and a greater world. Being chosen as a Light Warrior is based on three things; first a life's intention (path) dedicated to **Light**, second is taking personal responsibility by overcoming blame and stepping forward with the courage of a **Warrior**, and third, letting the **Heart** be your guide. 1. Light, 2. Warrior, 3. of the Heart, this is the Third Millennium Warrior. You have been chosen to take a seat among other Defenders of Light in a ceremony. This ceremony will give each warrior an opportunity to share individual experiences and culminating these pieces of knowledge in a grand collective puzzle (sacred gathering). Along with this exchange, each member will speak, instruct and participate in a culturally rich multi-disciplined spiritual event designed to challenge and to unify. We welcome you to step forward as a leader to recognize the Sacred Gathering that is happening here and now all around our planet. We welcome you to step forward as a leader and share what you intend to bring to this worldwide Sacred Gathering. If you accept this challenge, we will create the circle in **Darkness** and battle through the night until we reach the **Light** of day. An individual path has been recognized:

Way of the _____ **or a path as you define it**

_All that's required is commitment. To accept this challenge please contact _____ as soon as possible to add your path to the evening's agenda._

LESSON SEVENTY-EIGHT

The Process and the Path

Enlightened Journey

In western ideology, the principal focus to determine data is called, "the bottom line." At the end of a game the final scores are tallied, and this determines the winners and losers of the day. However, the games we play are only a microcosm of the grand universe, because the true game is life, and the game is not over. People tend to use this bottom line mentality to justify judgment. Judgment represents a conclusion that is predominantly determined by intellect rather than the heart. It is much easier to pass judgment than to seek compassion. Judgment, unfortunately, has its misconceptions because we are not the people that we used to be. We are not even the people that we think we are right now, but **we are the people that we are now becoming**. Sometimes it is necessary to recall a truth just to secure a place to begin again. Getting to the bottom of the truth does comply with western thinking. Life, however, is a process of lessons and this process is our journey through information. If you turn to the back of a book to get its message, or speed read passed the emotion then you have chosen to live only a small portion of the journey. The Culture of the Forgotten Truth teaches us to deny the process, but by doing so we can deny ourselves the miracle of the message. Become the question, become the process and as a result become the answer. Therefore, the afflicted can become the healer. It is experience that is the working formula for truth. Experience allows us to learn and to absorb information. The absorption of information takes us beyond the intellect. In Lao Tsu's *Tao Te Ching,* it is written, "The Tao that can be told is not the eternal Tao." The *Tao* is only one example of how the process teaches beyond the words by engaging spirit within the process. There are many other examples such as the philosophy of Zen. Zen is without thought process. It is based on an emptiness of mind only achieved through the constant practice of letting go. Another example of process is the Martial Arts. Repetition is what forges a martial artist into understanding. Yoga or Meditation is a state of consciousness understood only by those who engage their peace. The teachings of Christianity delivered through the New Testament of the Bible are a good example of process. The beloved result of this reading experience is the transformation of the seeker into a compassionate and forgiving person. Is it really the words on the page or is it the miracle of the message absorbed from the experience? A single phrase plucked from the Bible has small merit in comparison to the process of absorbing the message through time and diligent study. So many people will devote countless hours and energy to the study of the Bible and expect newcomers to get it all in a quick spoken phrase. If indeed a single quote from scripture is used to launch a righteous attack, then the message of compassion is lost or contradicted. The value of the process lies in the miracle of the message. Judgment must be channeled through the heart to achieve true justice. Only shallow imaginations from shortsighted visionaries would find bigotry in a message about compassion and forgiveness and yet, many people do.

Code of the Third Millennium Warrior is not a conclusion but a process. Doing and achieving become the same thing as the eastern and western ideals intertwine in a much more graceful strategy of one's daily accomplishments. Learn the Warriors Code, embrace it and then discipline it until you are the Warriors Code, and therefore do not need it. Take from it what you are willing to accept. It will serve you if you are willing to serve yourself. It is a philosophy that can be attached to all love-based beliefs. The journey is yours and this manuscript was created to help you along the way. You too have a message and a process. Your trials and tribulations serve you in delivering that message. Do not allow yourself to be defined by judgmental people. We are all becoming who we are striving to be. Turn your face to the beauty of humanity and may love and light shine bravely as the brightest star.

The Master's Path

Within every person exists a Master. It is a distant voice calling you and instructing you to look beyond the physical, beyond the practical, and beyond the emotional. This voice is mostly heard in stillness, yet when fully embraced, it can be heard in the midst of chaos. It has been called many things such as spirit, teacher, guardian, guide or soul. It is many things, and you need only apply your creativity to the image that is most pleasant for you. It is not necessary that we synchronize our images of divine purity; it is only necessary that we synchronize the essence of that purity. The essence is where answers exist. Images and names for spirituality continually create separation. This is a battle of words. Words are artistic tools to be shaped to the liking of the warrior poet. Creative differences are the basis for arguments concerning creation that breed religious wars against each other. How you choose to define the Master within is never as relevant as it is that you listen. **The Master within is guiding you on a path.** This is a higher path and soul's journey. This is a journey that the Light Warrior has begun and is not afraid to complete. In this lesson a design is created to reveal a map of the Master's Path in order to aid you in recognizing your potential toward Mastery work. It may seem simple, and it is supposed to be. It is the simple truth that awakens us when we have been sleeping.

1. **Creation**: *Birthing*: The beginning of a concept or a birthing of life, the beginning of form. In the beginning the child is nurtured into the realization of the real self and real *creativity*. Free-will begins development. This begins before your day of delivery.

2. **Self**: *Individuality*: "Who I am" emerges with the realization of the self-image from which all information is transmitted. Moralities and convictions come forth along with your personality. This is where you will define the Light or Dark of your ego. A strong *self awareness* and presence is attained in the development of this level of mastery.

3. **Warrior**: *Dragon Slayer, the seeker, and the hunter*: Here the self transforms into a *warrior of the self* and rises above the immature to achieve responsibility and personal power. This is the level of mastery in which fear, victimization and addiction are faced with victorious intent. Here you overcome blame in your life and move forward with a strength to choose whom you want and need to be. It is here that the warrior-self seeks out one's true purpose.

4. **Healer**: *Light Warrior, humanitarian, compassionate heart, the healer and giver*: This is the level at which the warrior of self learns the great power of surrender and allows love to guide the way by opening the heart and transforming the warrior of self into a **Warrior of the Heart**. Compassion, love and healing power illuminate at this level of mastery. The healing power breeds a shape shifting ability that can be refined.

5. **Messenger**: *Warrior Priest or Priestess*: The evolved Light Warrior, the teacher, shape-shifter, Shaman, the voice and vibration of Truth and neutralization. Here the presents of peace and power are clear. Allowing the master within to come forward, be heard, expressed and shared on a grander level of community reveals higher powers of expression.

6. **Peacemaker**: *Ambassador of Light, visionary and clairvoyant:* the sight, voice, heart and will of higher evolution illuminate together. This level can cross religions and philosophies. This is the power to neutralize War, Famine, or Disease. This is the level of the chosen

few. Those chosen must accept and choose leadership responsibilities on a global level.

7. **Master of Light**: *Mastery, Cosmic Union, Ascension, Enlightenment:* This is not the physical world, but is the ascension from the physical to the *spiritual consciousness.* This is mankind's highest achievement. This is the purest victory of freedom. The **Peacemaker** sees it, the **Messenger** voices it, the **Healer** feels it, and the **Warrior** of **Self** determines that it will be **Created**.

The Master's Path is based on the seven universal energy centers (chakras). Opening these chakras will aid you in hearing more candidly the voice of clarity within. The seven levels of Mastery transcend one from creation to creation, a **Circle of Light**. If one level is denied the circle will continue to perpetuate itself through many lifetimes until you experience your destiny.

CLOSING

My name is Michael Colley. I wrote this manuscript to the best of my abilities with the intention that it would help people. This undertaking took on its own voice. It was not written with the idea that I am the source of its information. This entire manuscript was writing from what I call a whisper in my ear. It is not an easy thing to admit to hearing voices and yet, I grew to know this whisper as a teacher, a warrior, a kind heart and a friend. I stayed as true to this message as humanly possible. From lesson one to lesson seventy-eight, nowhere do I refer to myself as the messenger. This is important to know because the message is far greater than I am.

On my thirty-seventh birthday, I began to document a personal journal and training log. It is written in the third person so I could share the journey as it was shared with me. The writing style has my influence, but my influence was always in close scrutiny. There are many ideas that are repeated and sometimes even sculpted. This is because it was only after many times explained would I finally understand that the messages would intertwine and be absorbed. As I grew in my training with the code I was able to grow in so many other areas of my life, including my career as an artist, my skill as a teacher and all my relationships across the board.

Even though I wrote these words, I still refer back to them for guidance on daily issues. It has taken my life to higher levels of integrity and changed the way I have grown to respect myself and others. There were even times when I wrote a complete lesson, read it the next day and not recall a word of it. I have learned so much from this manuscript that to this day, even though I wrote it without a writing partner, I still feel uncomfortable putting my name on the front as the author. The manuscript is not about me and wasn't meant to be. Please understand it was never my desire to share my personal experiences or relationship with this whisper in my ear, although after much deliberation, I felt this one vision needed to be conveyed. The following part of the manuscript is just one account of the many miraculous events that occurred during its writing. This story is about a storm that is coming. I felt I should share it.

I had been writing religiously for months on this manuscript when one day I began to question why all this was necessary. I was hearing more and more about this Army of Light, but had not understood the necessity of the message. That evening, I went for my three mile run on a beautiful sunny day. Off in the distance I saw storm clouds, but they were way too far to be of any concern. So I went about my run. By my halfway point with a mile and a half to go, the storm moved in so fast that rain and hail began coming down hard. This all occurred in about ten minutes. By the time I reached my car I was soaked and getting cold. I went to dinner with my fiancé that night and noticed I was not feeling well. By midnight my temperature was a hundred and three. What came next was a series of visions that changed the course of my understanding. As my temperature rose, I passed out and embarked on a night filled with several visionary journeys. It is important that you know, I witnessed this particular vision from a fever of extreme heat. For some of you this may be explained pragmatically as a fever induced delusion. However, I came to realize it was necessary for the question that I had asked be explained. Asking a question and getting the response became normality in my life. "Why was an Army of Light necessary?" This was the response.

At first, the night's pain and suffering was my closest companion. Then I was peacefully carried away to a far place in the distance. I observed a greatness that even a self-proclaimed warrior must respectfully acknowledge as humbling. It was like an ocean of blackness, an Ocean of Evil, so vast that the horizon extended beyond my furthest comprehension. It was if a shadow had consumed a part of the planet. It was the essence of evil and I could feel it. A single soul, even a warrior's soul, could easily be swept away in its depth and seduction. I hovered over it, never touching the black liquid-like substance, knowing all the while that I was being protected. The Black Ocean became aware I was there but did not move toward me. I felt as if I was not alone and was being held in a protected embrace. I was guided over it until I could consciously grasp both its hunger and its power. Its difficult to explain but somehow, I understood it had been feeding and patiently waiting, one soul at a time. This ocean was so vast and so deep that one man or one woman seems to be as insignificant as a raindrop hitting the ocean's surface miles out from shore. I then came to understand that this was the reality for the Light Warrior to take heed, because it has grown stronger than we know. Soul by soul, opportunity after opportunity, it gathers its power from fear and rage or the sufferings of others. It bides its time. It was coming and it was growing. When the evil is ready to strike, the cut will be clean and deep because the plan is patient and has been progressing for thousands of years. I was then able to realize its not about me its about all of us. The night was long, and I experienced several visions including warriors attacking out of a blaze of fire that could not be avoided and demons with powerful destructive ability that could seek you out even if you are hiding. If this sounds like a nightmare its because it was humanity dying. It was labeled an Epitaph of Shame.

I awoke the next morning crying and soaked in water from tears and sweat. From my bed I could see the storm was moving away and the sun was coming out. I also noticed that although a little dehydrated I rose out of bed perfectly fit, healthy and capable of having a productive day. From the question the morning before to the answer took a twenty-four hour cycle. It occurred to me later, sharing this personal vision was a responsibility. So here I am tonight on my fortieth birthday. I now turn the last page that concludes my three-year journal.

Together on this night,
the Light battled down the Dark
until it surrendered the day.
November 2, 2000

*Whether it be as a result of this manuscript, or not,
for those of you who put forth the effort to be a
good human being, I just wanted to say
THANK YOU.*

Michael Colley